THE
DICKENS ADVERTISER

A COLLECTION OF THE ADVERTISEMENTS IN THE
ORIGINAL PARTS OF NOVELS BY

CHARLES DICKENS

EDITED BY

BERNARD DARWIN

HASKELL HOUSE PUBLISHERS LTD.

Publishers of Scarce Scholarly Books

NEW YORK, N. Y. 10012

First Published 1930

HASKELL HOUSE PUBLISHERS LTD.
Publishers of Scarce Scholarly Books
280 LAFAYETTE STREET
NEW YORK. N. Y. 10012

Library of Congress Catalog Card Number: 72-155253

Standard Book Number 8383-1234-9

Printed in the United States of America

PREFATORY NOTE

THE object of this book is to reproduce some of the more entertaining advertisements that appeared in various of Dickens's novels, as they were published in their original monthly parts. The notion was not my own but that of a friend whose sense of humour was fired by a casual glance at some of those precious green numbers. The carrying out of it has been to some extent what Mr. Tony Weller called the pursuit of knowledge under difficulties since the original parts of Dickens are not easy to acquire; several kind people have however been good enough to entrust me with them. I am exceedingly thankful to them, and if possible still more thankful that I have now returned them their fragile and priceless possessions unscathed. I hope that these advertisements may amuse not only those who like everything to do with Dickens, but also some who are students of early-Victorianism and may like to see how the art of advertising has changed and progressed since Pickwick first burst on the world ninety-four years ago. Though their main object is to amuse yet perhaps they may also mildly instruct. The advertisements of our time will no doubt help the historians of the future to understand our everyday life and similarly these Dickens advertisements may throw for us some light on the whiskered ancestors and crinolined ancestresses therein depicted.

B. D.

CONTENTS

vii

THE
DICKENS ADVERTISER

CHAPTER I

THE ADVERTISERS OF THE DICKENSIAN ERA

THE advertiser of to-day probably regards with a good-natured contempt his predecessor of sixty and seventy years ago. His shop is the House of So-and-So, his goods are merchandise, and he disposes of them by an art called salesmanship, of which he speaks in a tone of awe and mystery. He is, in fact, a most genteel and superior person, and seems always to be saying with Mrs. Jarley, "It's calm and classical, that's what it is, calm and classical—no low beatings and knockings about, no jokings and squeakings like your precious Punches." He spends his splendid hundreds of thousands where his primitive forerunners spent but a few hundreds; and he knows no doubt a great deal more about the business than they ever did. Nevertheless, the productions of his genius will have perished utterly when theirs endure. His announcements sprawl over the pages of newspapers, and newspapers live only for a day, as the linings of drawers or in some forgotten portmanteau languishing in a dusty box room. Theirs will survive because they were made not in the mortal newspaper but in the immortal book. Consequently if they chose the right book their names will not be lost "for evermoe." Some future historian of the domestic life of the nineteenth century will know all about Morison and Lamplough, and will scarcely have heard, for all their noise, of Beecham and Eno; the dullest little statement in the smudgiest, tiniest little print about fenders, stoves and fire-irons will outlive even the sparkling dialogue of Mr. Everyman and Mr. Drage.

There cannot be any richer repository of these old advertisements, just as there cannot have been any better medium for them when they were new, than the numbers in which the Dickens books appeared. Month after month out came the eagerly expected number in its green cover, with the next instalment; and month after month the poetical Mr. Moses had a new poem about his wardrobe on the back of the cover, and the Gentleman's Real Head of Hair or Invisible Peruke occupied its modest fraction of a page at the beginning. The print may have been small; the advertisers may have known little about spacing and the use of bold letterings; their testimonials may have come only from a legendary Mrs.—— and not from famous actresses or cricketers, but they have built themselves a monument more enduring than have the brazen trumpeters of a later time.

It is to be hoped that Dickens himself found these advertisements as engaging as we do now. He ought to have done so, for he was a showman himself, always keeping an eye on that public of which he regarded himself as the servant. His motto was Mrs. Jarley's, " The people expect it of me and public characters can't be their own masters and mistresses." Not disdaining the art of showmanship in his own case, he had the keenest appreciation of it in the case of other people, and if he enjoyed the giant inside the caravan, he relished quite as delightedly the picture outside depicting him as

rather larger than he really was. In *Pickwick* the
practical side of advertising is well illustrated by
Mr. Bob Sawyer when he set up for himself at
Bristol. "The lamplighter has eighteen pence a
week to pull the night bell for ten minutes every
time he comes round; and my boy always rushes
into church just before the psalms, when the people
have got nothing to do but look about 'em, and calls
me out with horror and dismay depicted on his
countenance. 'Bless my soul,' everybody says,
'somebody taken suddenly ill.' Sawyer, late
Nockemorf, sent for, what a business that young
man has."

In *Nicholas Nickleby*, which came next but one
in order, we find two distinguished advertisers, one
on the literary and one on the practical side. Mr.
Squeers confined himself to his one famous announcement as to the delightful village of Dotheboys, near
Greta Bridge, in Yorkshire, too famous to quote.
Mr. Vincent Crummles was a master of all the arts
of publicity, and attended Miss Petowker's wedding
in the part of the bride's father, in a brown George
wig, a seventeenth century snuff-coloured suit,
buckled shoes and a flood of tears. In *Martin
Chuzzlewit*, Mr. Pecksniff's advertisement for a new
pupil was as eloquent as Mr. Squeers's, and Mr.
Montague Tigg and the Anglo-Bengalee were a
triumph of showmanship, but the greatest advertiser,
or at any rate the one of whose art we are told in
greatest detail, was Mrs. Jarley. She held decided
views as to the effectiveness of different methods.
As to poetry she said, "It comes so very expensive
and I really don't think it does much good," but
perhaps this was only in order to beat down the
poet as to his price; she gave three and sixpence instead of the demanded five shillings, for
Mr. Slum's acrostic which was intended for
Warren's blacking, but was convertible to Jarley.
She was quite clear in her mind as to the nature

of the appeal to be made to different classes. The handbills with:

"If I know'd a donkey wot wouldn't go
To see Mrs. Jarley's wax-work show "

were only distributed to taverns. They were to please the lawyers' clerks, whereas Mr. Slum's acrostic, with "over the water to Jarley," and " I saw thy show in youthful prime," was allowed to penetrate to the more refined atmosphere of the home. The boarding schools for young ladies had other handbills specially composed for them. When the more likely customers had spent their money Mrs. Jarley recognized that a special campaign must be undertaken, "For," as she observed, "now that the schools are gone and the regular sightseers exhausted, we come to the general public, and they want stimulating." She appreciated the advertising value of Little Nell, and sent her out with the wax Brigand in a light cart decorated with flags, and then, the desired impression having been made, sent the Brigand out by himself again lest Little Nell should become too cheap. Even to-day the zealous young student of showmanship might do worse than analyse thoroughly Mrs. Jarley's precepts and methods.

There are other instances that might be quoted. At any rate, Dickens loved a good advertiser, and I hope and believe that he read all the advertisements that appeared in every monthly part of his books.

There are no advertisements on the front of the cover. That is always taken up by a composite design showing, as a rule, the characters and incidents of the story, such as the picture on the outside of *Edwin Drood,* which has been used by the various schools of thought as evidence in support of their theories as to the end of the story. The back of the cover, on the other hand, must have been greatly coveted, and it was here that Mr. Moses, the tailor, printed some of his delightful poems which will have a chapter all to themselves. Inside the cover there is a number of pages both at the beginning and the end, between which the instalment of the story is sandwiched, and each series is headed, " Dombey and Son Advertiser. No. XVI. January, 1848", or as the case may be. The pages are small and narrow, and there is therefore little opportunity for that bold spacing and impressively large lettering which the advertiser of to-day would desire. Indeed, the advertisements give the impression of being bunched and cramped into an insufficient space, and the print is often abominably small. Those who designed them must have had a great belief in the reader's curiosity and power of wading through an unrelieved mass of statements in infamous type. The pictures are nearly always most engaging, but some of the unillustrated pages have a forbidding air. There are gems of purest ray to be found concealed in them, but they need more finding than the average reader would, as one might suppose, have been ready to give them. If we have gout because our grandfathers drank too much port wine, I am sure we must wear spectacles because they read too small print.

Those little huddled paragraphs make a good point from which to embark on a sea of speculation as to ancient and modern advertising. They may mean only that, as anyone can see, the pages were small, and there was no room for generous display. On the other hand, they mean something much more significant, namely that the advertiser did not yet understand the tremendous power that he was wielding. Like Mrs. Jarley, in the case of poetry, he may still have thought that it did not do much good, so that he needed much stimulating to make him advertise at all; when he did take the plunge he did it only half-heartedly, spending his money in the most cautious driblets. Consequently, he had so much to say in his little space that he had to say it in small crowded type. If that was so it seems to us now that he was stupid, that he ought to have realized that a few big words catching the eye were worth more than a crowd of words looking utterly dull and insignificant. In some cases, at any rate, it cannot have been economy which was at the bottom of it. Some advertisers took up several pages, or had special pamphlets sewn in for them, so that they had plenty of room, and yet each page was full to overflowing, and there was nothing but a mass of unchanging small type, which repelled instead of attracted the reader, and, like Lant Street in the Borough, shed a gentle melancholy upon the soul. Here surely the cause must have been sheer lack of imagination on the advertiser's part, and nothing else. He cannot have thought that anyone would wade through that mass of words, those rows of tiny little testimonials from Mr. A—— or Mr. B——; unless he believed that the reader would be simply overpowered by numbers and yield under this show of the colossal, it is hard to understand his frame of mind.

It may be, of course, that in saying this we have forgotten one important fact, namely, that the advertisers and their readers were Victorian and that we are not. We may be flippant, easily bored, living or pretending to live at a wild and hustling pace, beginning many things and going through with but few of them. They, on the other hand, may have been full of greater, if possibly more tiresome qualities, with a moral earnestness, a determination to be interested in all sorts of dreadfully dull things and plenty of time to do it in. I cannot say I wholly believe in this explanation, but I put it tentatively forward. Occasionally in reading through these advertisements I have believed in it altogether.

The most convincing piece of testimony is provided by the pamphlets issued by the National Anti-Corn Law League, and sewn into various numbers of *Martin Chuzzlewit*. Like the church in Congreve's poem, they "Strike an awe and terror on my aching sight." Eight solid pages there are, and to read all of them would be a nightmare comparable only to a railway journey with Uncle Joseph Finsbury, from *The Wrong Box*.

The longest and dullest pamphlet is supposed to represent a conversation that takes place on a steamboat between a Gentleman and a Farmer. "Good morning, Sir," says the Gentleman, "I see you have the *Mark Lane Express* in your hand; how do they quote the price of corn to-day?" and then they go at it hammer and tongs, though each is exceedingly polite to the other, and always prefaces his remarks with "Well, that is very fairly stated." About seventy-five per cent. of the talking is done by the Gentleman, and it is small wonder that the poor Farmer says, "I like to hear you talk, and yet I don't like to hear you, if you can make that out." The second part of his observation we can make out easily enough, but "the conversation was only interrupted by the termination of the voyage." It is of a tediousness that no words can describe, even when it has a spice of the archaic and the absurd to cheer us. And yet, presumably, many ardent followers of Mr. Cobden and Mr. Bright read it all, and the succeeding pamphlets as well. Or did they only pretend to do so with an immoral earnestness?

To return to the little paragraphs, with their testimonials, it is noticeable that they are all or very nearly all from quite obscure persons. To-day happy vendors can always get celebrities to praise their wares, though whether they pay them to do it and if so how much is a sacred mystery. In the Dickens advertisers we cannot find so much as an actress or a lord. There are, of course, plenty of allusions to royalty, nobility and gentry, but they are all perfectly vague, except that Lea & Perrins do give the coat of arms of the " nobleman in the county " from whom came the recipe for Worcester sauce.

Our modern ready-made tailors dress cricketers and jockeys in their suits and photograph them thus adorned, but Mr. Moses never gave a suit away to anybody, or never mentioned it if he did. Was this economy, or had he never thought of it, or would the celebrity have refused the suit if he had? Probably Victorian celebrities were more dignified than ours are, and would have scorned the action. If so, there is a good deal to be said for their point of view.

To say of the writers of testimonials that they were humble and obscure might be insulting to-day. It does not seem so when we are reading the Dickens advertisers, because the advertisements there not merely take differences of social status as a matter of course, but almost go out of their way to insist on them. Different wares are said to be suited to the peer, the merchant, the shop-keeper and the workman respectively. Mr. Moses told his prospective customer that if he bought his clothes at Aldgate he would, when he got to his watering-place, look just like the members of the fashionable throng he would find there. His counterpart of to-day would assume that the customer was himself a fashionable; he calls everybody " My lord " as did the pea-and-thimble man in *Lavengro*. Those who nowadays want to sell us furniture on the hire purchase system do hint at the fact that we are not very rich, that we have to work for our living, and may lose our job, but they do it with infinite delicacy. We may, in fact, live in a small house in the suburbs, but it is somehow flatteringly implied that if we liked we might be furnishing a "mansion" instead.

It seems rather odd and unadventurous in the advertisers of Dickens's day that they made so little use of Dickens himself. To-day he is constantly used, and the learned editor of *The Dickensian* has made a large collection of such advertisements. A picture of Captain Cuttle with a clay pipe is an advertisement of tobacco; Mr. Turveydrop making his high-shouldered bow to Esther at the dancing academy represents a famous polish; Mr. Micawber and Sam Weller appear at regular intervals. Yet when Dickens was at the very height of his fame, when it must be regretfully admitted that there were more people than there are now who could pass an examination in Captain Cuttle or Mr. Turveydrop, the value of Dickens's characters as advertisements does not seem to have struck anyone. Mr. Pickwick was an exception. We know that when the tremendous popularity was surging in full tide many things were called after the great man. If we wanted to insult somebody's cigar even to-day we might call it a "Penny Pickwick" and if we were suddenly asked to quote an advertisement as to a nib we should instantly say:

> "They come as a boon and a blessing to men,
> The Pickwick, the Owl and the Waverley pen."

Unlike the Nickleby pen, long since dead, those two names have survived; probably neither were contemporary, and indeed Mr. Percy Fitzgerald, in his *History of Pickwick*, tells us that the cigar was not. Those that were have long since been forgotten. "Pickwick chintzes," says Mr. Fitzgerald, "figured in linen-drapers' windows, and Weller corduroys in breeches-makers' advertisements; Boz cabs might be seen rattling through the streets, and the portrait of the author of Pelham or Crichton was scraped down or pasted over to make room for that of the new popular favourite in

the omnibuses. There were to be seen Pickwick
canes, Pickwick gaiters, Pickwick hats, with narrow
curled brims; and even tobacco-stoppers." A more
alarming manifestation was the formation of Pickwick clubs, in which it appears that the members
supported the different characters in the book or
called themselves by their names. It is dreadful to
contemplate the depths of facetiousness to which they
must have descended. Hero-worship has its pitfalls,
and Dickensians, like all other "somethingeans,"
are apt to go too far. Even to-day there are "Mr.
Pickwick's old-fashioned Candies," though there is
as little evidence that Mr. Pickwick ever ate a candy
as that he smoked a cigar. The name Pickwick was
freely used but, except apparently for the Weller
corduroys, the names of the other characters were
not: still less were the characters themselves taken
and made to utter words in praise of somebody's
wares. "Let us have some of your best wine to-day,
waiter," said Mr. Wardle, with a delightful trust-
fulness, at Osborne's Hotel, in the Adelphi, and no
one thought of saying what was the brand which the
waiter brought. So far as I know, nobody claimed
to be Mr. Toots's tailor—surely a great opportunity
lost. The Christmas value of Dickens was not
appreciated, and altogether there was a lack of
invention and enterprise.

It may have been that the advertisers of those
days stuck more closely to business. They thought
that what they had to do was to talk exclusively
about their wares, and did not believe in dragging
Dickens or anyone else in by the heels. The modern
advertiser proceeds rather on Mr. Crummles's plan:
he has his piece written to fit the real pump and the
two washing tubs. He takes Dickens, and he takes
the thing he wants to sell, and the deuce is in it
if he cannot find some connecting link between them.
This plan has lately been carried to its extreme
limit by the parson of a Lincolnshire parish, who

appealed for funds to restore his church on the
ground that the son of Sergeant Bompas, the original
of Sergeant Buzfuz, was ordained there; I hope he
got, as Mr. Weller said of Messrs. Dodson and Fogg,
"a fat and happy livin' out of it." To be sure Mr.
Moses, of Aldgate, who really was an enterprising
person, and a poet into the bargain, did make some
use of Dickens. He made puns about a suit in
Chancery and a suit from his shop, and he used
the title of *Bleak House* to suggest the bitter weather
that only his overcoats could ward off. But then Mr.
Moses was in many ways ahead of his time. He
was the only person to see the value of light and
agreeable verse, and he ventured to make jokes.
He did not make too many, and they nearly always
took the form of elaborate plays upon words, but still
he was not too terribly serious.

Nobody else made jokes at all, and hardly anybody thought of having amusing pictures, though
many people had amusing pictures without thinking
of it. How amusing they were when they were
published we cannot now say. Did anyone smile
at the scenes of domestic bliss in which papa
and mama and the children are all revelling so
blamelessly in the Lenticular Stereoscope? Whiskers
as whiskers were not then the incentives to giggling
that they are now, but that Podsnappian father
could never have been taken quite seriously. And
yet there are gentlemen very like him still to be
found in certain catalogues. They are generally
playing some form of round game at Christmas
time, with a happy circle of young people, so that
apparently paterfamilias has remained for certain
purposes a more or less unchanging figure. It is,
perhaps, the best plan to enjoy his whiskers without
too close inquiry.

CHAPTER II

ANCIENT AND MODERN

WHETHER or not there really were in those dim ages papas who looked like Mr Podsnap, there were, at any rate, plenty who behaved like him. His views about not bringing the blush to the cheek of the young person are reflected in innumerable advertisements. The lady must be able to get into her carriage in her crinoline without inciting the onlookers to rude jests. French must be learnt without danger to morals, and it is the first requisite of any piece of literature that it can be admitted into the household without fear of consequences. Any other quality comes in a very bad second to respectability, and "in the belief that the heart needs to be educated to the full as much as the head, the constant aim has been to appeal to the feelings as well as the intellect. Prominence is given to none but the highest and tenderest feelings of humanity."

When a publisher brings out a translation of Eugene Sue's *Mysteries of Paris*, he probably wants the world to have hopes of some little French impropriety, but he nevertheless takes care to remark that the book " excludes everything which can by possibility be thought offensive to the English reader," who will be " excited and terrified but yet touched and refined."

Nevertheless, however flippantly we may snigger at the *Family Herald* and *Holy Homes*, we have to confess that they are in wonderfully good company.

If we imagine a match played between the books advertised in Dickens and those advertised in any and every way to-day, there would only be one side in it. The ancients would beat the moderns out of the field. They have such a team, with Shakespeare at the head of it, and Dickens himself and Thackeray for its young players, as never was seen. Those book advertisements ought to make us feel at least reasonably humble about the Victorians. Their liking for having illustrations to their books strikes us to-day as singular. We are ourselves fond of the Phiz pictures to our Dickens, because we have grown up with them, and can hardly imagine the books without them, but, generally speaking, we would much rather have our own ideas of the characters in books than anybody else's. People thought otherwise in Dickens's times; the illustrator was a very important person, and we ought to be glad that he was so, for we owe *Pickwick* to the fact that Dickens was engaged to do a piece of hack work in writing some kind of story round Seymour's plates.

The advertisements of music were far from living up to the standard of those of literature. I shall in the chapter on the Young Person quote some words from the songs in Jullien's Album, and they are of much the same quality as those into which Silas Wegg used to drop, as a friend, for the benefit of Mr. and Mrs. Boffin. A learned Dickens scholar, Mr. J. W. T. Ley, has lately been investigating Silas Wegg's poetry; he has published the results of his researches in *The Dickensian*, and I will venture to borrow a little from them. It would seem that on the whole Mr. Wegg quoted very accurately. There is, for instance, the poem "respecting the extent to which he would be willing to put himself out of the way to bring Mrs. Boffin round in case she ever got low in her spirits."

> I'll tell thee how the maiden wept, Mrs. Boffin,
>   When her true love was slain, ma'am,
> And how her broken spirit slept, Mrs. Boffin,
>   And never woke again, ma'am.
> I'll tell thee (if agreeable to Mr. Boffin) how the steed
>   draw nigh,
>   And left his lord afar;
> And if my tale (which I hope Mr. Boffin might excuse)
>   should make you sigh,
>   I'll strike the light guitar.

Stripped of the additions by which Mr. Wegg's genius turned the ridiculous into the sublime, that poem is almost word for word correct and "The Light Guitar" was, Mr. Ley says, often to be found in old albums.

> "Weep for the hour
>   When to Boffin's bower "

is Eveleen's Bower no more than reasonably mis-quoted.

> "And my eldest brother lean'd upon his sword, Mr. Boffin,
>   And wiped away a tear "

is exactly what the soldier did in "The Soldier's Tear."

> "A stranger to something and what's his name joy,
>   Behold little Edmund, the poor Peasant boy "

shows how great an improvement can be made by the slightest touch of a master hand, and all these songs would have found a perfectly appropriate home with Mr. Jullien.

There is one class of advertisement wholly absent from the Dickens books, namely that which shows the way to self-improvement for commercial ends. To-day we are bidden to study systems of training which will enable us to develop our personalities, dominate the society in which we move, and become energetic, resourceful and generally unpleasant persons, but the moral is always pointed for us by stories of students whose incomes increased by leaps and bounds. It is the same with those who are depicted studying book-keeping by double entry under a reading lamp when they might be idly amusing themselves at a picture palace after their day's work. We are invited to learn how to speak good English, and an awful warning is provided by a picture of a gentleman who has just lost his job. "Look at them people," he is saying bitterly, "I worked myself to death for them," and his wife, who presumably comes from America, answers, "We're surely up against hard luck." If the poor man had learnt to say, "Those people," he would be earning a princely and increasing salary.

The advertisers of Dickens's time were not so practically-minded. They urged the reader to buy Mr. Frith's beautiful picture of the "Village Pastor," not in order to earn £1,000 a year, but because Mr. Frith "had a great deal of sentiment fortunately based on the soundest principles of art." Perhaps an exception should be made in favour of Mr. Smart, who was ready to make his pupils "accomplished in the Caligraphic art." However old or young they may be, and however bad their writing, they might "in eight lessons acquire permanently an elegant and flowing style of penmanship adapted either to professional pursuits or private correspondence." He also taught book-keeping, shorthand and "arithmetic on a method requiring only one-third of the time and mental labour usually required." No doubt Mr. Smart meant to entrap the industrious young man who had had no advantages and wanted to get on in the world, but he thought it indelicate to say so, and cited no pupils who had attained to affluence. Perhaps the young men of the day agreed with Uriah Heep when he refused to be taught by David Copperfield, despite the difficulties of the Latin phrases in Mr. Tidd:

their betters resented too much learning, and to be humble was the way to get on. They were at any rate too humble to proclaim their own qualifications; or possibly they only did that in the Agony Column of the newspapers. The one exception was a young man who published in *Nicholas Nickleby* this announcement: "DOUCEUR! Five hundred pounds or more proportionally will be given to any influential Party who may introduce a Young Gentleman to a Respectable Permanent Appointment. Inviolate secrecy in every respect will be faithfully maintained."

If there is no evidence of the young man being urged to improve himself, so there is none, or very little, of his reprehensibly idling away his time at games and sports. To-day games come into all manner of advertisements. If a young man is trying on underclothing he has a golf club leaning against the wall; if he is drinking lemonade with a young lady they have just finished a set of lawn tennis, and at the end of an innings at cricket he is making a dash for beer. Long before that stage, when he has only just been rescued from the grave by somebody's infant food, he is kicking a football. In the Dickens advertisers he was very occasionally portrayed shooting or riding, but even so he was not young; he had by that time become the plump and prosperous merchant who could reasonably afford such indulgences. The only evidence available to a future historian that anybody ever played games or took any interest in out-of-door sports, except shooting and riding, is provided by a picture of a young lady playing croquet.

Yet there were, in those days, great men of the out-of-door world, at whose shrine worshippers prostrated themselves. There hangs over my chimney-piece a lithograph of George Frost, the Suffolk Stag, winning the Championship belt in a race on the Copenhagen Ground in 1853, the

year that *Bleak House* was published.   He is skim-
ming over the ground with a nonchalant grace,
much as did Mr. Pickwick when he ran home to
bed after falling through the ice, and it is on record
that thousands of copies of that lithograph were
sold—an honour that would not now be paid to
any runner.   It must be confessed that the Suffolk
Stag is not a good instance.   His name is clean
forgotten, or only remembered by those who, in
contradistinction to Mr. Blotton, of Aldgate, "culti-
vate the mysterious and the sublime."   There
were, however, others who are not yet forgotten.
Alfred Mynn was born only three years before
Dickens, and appeared at Lord's for the first time
five years before *Pickwick* was published.   He and
Fuller Pilch and the other members of the immortal
Kent eleven were at the height of their fame when
Dickens was at the height of his.   In the year
before that of *Our Mutual Friend* "W.G." himself
came up to London, as a boy of sixteen, to play
for the South Wales Club at the Oval, and he
was two and twenty when Dickens died.   The Ring
had long since passed its golden age and was sink-
ing into decadence, but Tom Sayers fought the
Benicia Boy in 1860.   Thackeray wrote an account
of the battle in the *Cornhill* and a poem about
it in *Punch*, and *The Times* received many anony-
mous contributions to a testimonial for the British
hero.   Yet, as far as the contemporary advertisements are concerned, these great men might
never have existed; they are represented only by
that lackadaisical young woman playing croquet,
holding her mallet with her hands the wrong way
up.
  For this state of things there must be various
reasons.   The interest in games was not by innumerable degrees so passionate or so general as
it is now; paragraphs were written about them
where there are now columns; Mynn was not

c

nearly so famous as Hobbs, and the time had not
quite come when crowds assembled at railway
stations to see W.G. passing through in his train
from Gloucester to smash the northern bowlers.
Games were still primarily amusements for boys,
not for grown-ups, and Mr. Podsnap had probably only the haziest recollections of having played
with hoops and marbles at school. Tom Sayers
was an exception; he must have been for a while
as popular a hero as ever lived, but he was wor-
shipped, as his battles were fought, under the
rose. He was presumably the subject only of
masculine conversation, and indeed I can remember an old gentleman who was telling me with the
greatest zest about Caunt and Bendigo on the
way upstairs from the dining-room, but stopped
abruptly as he opened the drawing-room door to
join the ladies. Sayers would never have been
depicted in the illustrated papers, as are his degen-
erate successors, playing games with his children.
He might, one would have supposed, without
shocking anybody unduly, have given a testimonial to a pill, but the personal touch and the
exploiting of famous characters of any kind were
still in their infancy. When all is said, however,
it is odd that not so much as a single child in a
juvenile tailor's advertisement has a bat in his
hand, or is even throwing a ball.

Our hypothetical historian of the future might
be led to think not only that people never played
games but that they never took holidays. Mr.
Moses, as I said before, alluded to one of his customers mingling with the fashionable throng at a
seaside resort, but the seaside resorts never thought
of advertising themselves, and their attractions.
There are a few announcements as to hotels at
such places as Bath and Leamington, and that is
all; neither coaches nor, later on, railway com-
panies told of the delightful places to which they

went: change of air was not considered a necessity of life and, since leaving home was a distinct undertaking, people stayed there very contentedly.

There is plenty of scope for inquiry as to why the sellers of certain particular goods were apparently so much more go-ahead than all the rest. Hair-oil, for instance, was freely advertised; there was not only Rowland with his Kalydor and Macassar oil, but various other minor luminaries. Soap, on the other hand, might hardly ever have been used for all we hear about it. The great Pears, who is sometimes said to have been the founder of modern advertising, appears quite late in the day, and then very modestly and tentatively, while none of his rivals follow his example. One might infer from this that it was the makers of luxuries who were the earliest to grasp the value of advertising, whereas those who made necessaries had not got past the point of thinking that people must buy their wares whatever happened. The very rare advertisements of such things as mustard and beer and tooth powder might be held to bear this out, but the generalization is a rash one. The one tradesman above all others who had discovered what could be done by blowing his own trumpet was the maker of pills. He was fully as confident, as brazen, and as comprehensive in his promises as are any of his successors, though sometimes rather less delicate in his language. Probably he found a readier market than he does now, for there were no new-fangled notions as to curing people by starving them or making them live in the open air; physic reigned supreme, and the world said to its sick people, "You come and be dosed," as Mrs. Joe Gargery did to Pip before administering tar-water. The most blatant of modern pill-men would hardly venture to recommend his pills as a cure for the smallpox as Morison did, stating that two patients ate and drank whatever they pleased throughout their illness and were quite free from any fever.

There is, at any rate, one other thing that we can hardly conceive any advertiser doing to-day, and that is the publishing of an imaginary conversation in which the Sovereign takes part. Yet there is such a scene, with Queen Victoria in the leading part, in the Nickleby Advertiser of April 1, 1839. It was apparently reprinted from *The Mirror of Parliament* of some little time before, and its object was to make people sign a petition for the penny post as proposed by Rowland Hill. It begins with all proper stage directions. Council ·Chamber in Windsor Castle.

Her Majesty is sitting at a large table, on which are lying Reports on Postage. Her Majesty is in deep study over ' Post Office Reform' by Rowland Hill. Lord Melbourne at the Queen's right hand is watching Her Majesty's countenance.

THE QUEEN (*exclaiming aloud*). Mothers pawning their clothes to pay the postage of a child's letter! Every subject studying how to evade postage, without caring for the law! Even Messrs. Baring sending letters illegally every week to save postage! Such things must not last. (*To* LORD MELBOURNE) I trust, my Lord, you have commanded the attendance of the Post Master General and Mr. Rowland Hill, as I directed, in order that I may hear the reasons of both about this Universal Penny Postage Plan, which appears to me likely to remove all these great evils. Moreover, I have made up my mind that the three hundred and twenty petitions presented to the House of Commons during the last session of Parliament, which pray for a fair trial of the plan, shall be at least attended to. (*A pause.*) Are you, my Lord, yourself, able to say anything about this postage plan, which all the country seems to be talking about?

LORD MELBOURNE. May it please Your Majesty, I have heard something about it, but——

THE QUEEN. Heard! So I suppose has everyone from the Land's End to John o' Groats' house. I wish to learn what your Lordship thinks of it.

LORD MELBOURNE (*aside*). I really think nothing, because I know nothing. May it please Your Majesty, the Post Master General tells me the plan will not do, and that, to confess the truth, is all I know about the matter.

Enter Groom of the Chambers.

GROOM. The Post Master General and Mr. Rowland Hill await Your Majesty's pleasure.
THE QUEEN. Give them entrance.

(*Enter* LORD LICHFIELD *and* MR. ROWLAND HILL.)

THE QUEEN. I am happy to see my noble Post Master General and the ingenious author of this Universal Penny Postage Plan. Gentlemen, be seated."

After this Mr. Hill argues convincingly and Lord Lichfield shuffles under the Queen's severe cross-examination until he says at last,

"Please, Your Majesty, I feel very uneasy."
THE QUEEN. "Support his Lordship, my Lord Melbourne."
LORD LICHFIELD. "With Your Majesty's leave, I will retire."

The Queen then declares that Lord Lichfield must go, and Lord Melbourne basely deserts him and admits that as a Post Master General he "has not realized the fond hopes we cherished of him."

Finally the Queen rises and in a most emphatic tone says that she "agrees with her faithful Commons in recommending a uniform penny post, and that if he cannot find a minister to do it she will find one herself." Exit the Queen, Lord Melbourne and Mr. Rowland Hill bowing.

Some three months later, on July 12, Penny Postage being included in the budget was carried in the House of Commons.

The reader will be able to judge for himself, from the samples given, the literary style of the advertisers. It is a style of grandiloquence rising often to the heights of pomposity. Two at least of Dickens's characters would have been masters of it, Mr. Micawber and Mr. Pott, the editor of the Eatanswill Gazette. Mr. Micawber had the flow of solemn and sonorous language with an added touch of picturesqueness and colour that would have put him in a class of his own when nothing but ecstatic praise was required. Mr. Pott—and for that matter Mr. Slurk also—would have been called in when it was necessary for the seller not merely to laud his wares but to heap abuse on a rival. This the Dickensian advertisers were fond of doing; they seemed to live in a state of bitter hostility towards some "party," who had infringed their rights and imitated their goods. The challenge to the law-courts trembled perpetually on their lips and was only with-held because the hated rival's efforts had so dismally and deservedly failed.

The Eatanswill Gazette predicted that Mrs. Leo Hunter's party "would present a scene of varied and delicious enchantment—a bewildering coruscation of beauty and talent—a lavish and prodigal display of hospitality—above all, a degree of splendour softened by the most exquisite taste; and adornment refined with perfect harmony and the chastest good keeping—compared with which, the fabled gorgeousness of Eastern Fairyland itself would appear to be clothed in as many dark and murky colours, as must be the mind of the splenetic and unmanly being who could presume to taint with the venom of his envy, the preparations made by the virtuous and highly distinguished lady, at whose shrine this humble tribute of admiration was offered." That passage, which I could not deny myself the sensual pleasure of transcribing, is an almost perfect parody of the Dickensian style and language of advertising.

Compare with it for example this genuine specimen headed "Elegance and Economy for the Table," about Watson's New Albata Plate. "C. Watson begs the Public will understand that this Metal is peculiarly his own, and that Silver is not more different from Gold, than *his* Metal is from all others; the Public will therefore have no difficulty in discovering the animus which directs the virulent attacks made against him, by a party who is daily suffering from the unparalleled success which has marked the progress of his New Plate since its introduction. C.W., unlike this *party*, courts comparison, feeling confident that the result will establish its pre-eminence."

That is a particularly fine specimen ·because it shows the advertiser describing himself by his initials. "C.W. courts comparison." "J.I. and Co. were induced." "E.M. and Son have made arrangements"—this is a modest style that has to-day disappeared, in favour of "The House of So and So," and the change is all for the worse. So is the change whereby tradesmen now treat their competitors with silent contempt instead of blackguarding them picturesquely. Listen to Mr. Harris, the Optician, in the fifth number of *Dombey*, "CAUTION. To prevent mistakes, the public are requested to notice the name *Thomas Harris* and Son and the number (52) is laid in *Mosaic Pavement* on the footway contiguous to their shop. Attention to this Caution is necessary to prevent mistakes in consequent of the *unprincipled* conduct of a person in the immediate neighbourhood." To-day nobody rises beyond a lukewarm and anæmic caution to the buyer to reject imitations.

It is fair to say that the advertisers were not always boiling with rage and overflowing with venom. "The coming festivities of the races, the drawing-rooms given by our youthful and beloved Sovereign and the fêtes and parties of our nobility will contribute to the desired result and the purveyors to luxury and taste are making every provision for the anticipated demand." In that passage there is no trace of any sentiment save a bland self-satisfaction. Incidentally as it was published at the date of *Edwin Drood* when Queen Victoria had already been on the throne some three and thirty years, the writer had claims to be considered a courtier.

Mr. Micawber might have written it, but here is another passage perhaps more characteristic of him; he loved an allusion as to the gowans in "Auld Lang Syne", though he was not precisely aware what they might be, and this advertisement—of Gilbert's Atlas—is full of romantic allusions. "If all persons could once be led to this, it is incalculable to conceive how much more delightful it would make the world we live in; because it would enable us to live mentally, and in our mental life consists our real enjoyment of all the world at once. Thus, for instance, we should be enabled to drink our coffee in the Groves of Yemen, with turbaned Arabs and loaded camels around us, and under that balmy sky, we could look across the Red Sea, where there is in one place an assemblage of worm-built reefs, extending line upon line, and white with the foam produced by an angry wind; and another place reeking with the steam of volcanic fires, while the bottom is as gay as a garden with the vegetation of the deep, and the waters are literally encumbered with living creatures. So might we drink our tea in some fantastic alcove of a Chinese mandarin, and enjoy the characters of that most singular country, which has remained changeless for hundreds of years. We should never taste the stimulating flavour of Cinnamon without being borne in thought to Ceylon, with its rich fields of rice, its beautiful copses, which furnish this exhilarating spice; its tangled and swampy woods, with their herds of gigantic elephants; its more dry and inlaced forests, peopled with countless thousands of apes, which make the early morn hideous with their cries. So also, we should never taste a clove or a nutmeg, without being wafted to the spicy islands of the oriental Archipelago, where all is the vigour and growth and beauty and the richness of perfume. But we must stop, for there is no end to the catalogue, and it is an

exhibition of which we must not see too much at
a passing glance, lest it should wile us from our
proper purpose. And we have mentioned these
few particulars merely to let those who are yet in
ignorance of the subject know how well the world
is worth our studying; how richly the earth which
we inhabit has been endowed by its bountiful
Maker; how full the feast which it affords to all;
and yet how varied, how free from surfeiting, how
healthful."

With this prospectus of an Atlas we may compare one of a work on travel in *Martin Chuzzlewit*,
because the same theme is here treated in super-
ficially the same way but yet with a touch of lightness which becomes almost frivolity. The book is
The Library of Travel. Edited by Walter K. Kelly
and Son, and published by Chapman and Hall.

"The mania for wandering is no longer confined
to the English people; other nations have caught
the infection, and the symptoms find utterance in
all the tongues of the West. The earnest German
carries far abroad his patient spirit of research,
and his old-world thoughtfulness and depth of
feeling; the fluent Frenchman, in canary-coloured
gloves, rhapsodizes about 'la belle France' amidst
the awful relics and the living glories of the East;
and our American cousin cries 'Go ahead!' to all
the echoes of the earth." The epithet "earnest"
has to-day become one of mockery, but it was not
so when that passage was written, and that the
writer should smile at the German for his earnestness shows a daring and flippancy quite remarkable.

CHAPTER III

PICKWICK is among Dickens's books so much a thing apart that it must have a chapter to itself. To look to-day at the advertisements in those slim engaging green numbers is to see at a glance how the fame of the author grew. To begin with, Seymour's plates were supposed to be the chief attraction and, popular though he no doubt was, Seymour by himself was not enough to attract many advertisements. After he was dead, and, when Sam Weller made his bow in the fourth number, the great tide of popularity rose and rose, the pillmakers and hairdressers and booksellers awoke and poured in their advertisements. With Sam's advent there began the Pickwick Advertiser, of which twenty thousand copies were ultimately printed and sewn into the numbers.

In the copy of *Pickwick* which I was lucky enough to borrow the Advertiser does not appear till a good deal later. This is an odd state of things, and the question of the particular advertisements in any particular number is a most recondite one upon which collectors spend treasures of learning. It is too deep for me to attempt to elucidate it. Here is what an erudite American author says, in discussing the points essential to a perfect copy of *Pickwick*. "After all the chief conflicts are centred on the advertisements as they appeared and were omitted in the earlier parts. This was the restless and uncertain age of *Pickwick*. Due to the

26

phenomenal increase in circulation there came new advertising material, together with substitutions and cancellation. Under such conditions confusion resulted. Following the sixth part the advertising became somewhat crystallized, and radical changes have not been so apparent." It is all rather confusing, but presumably more and more copies of numbers were reprinted as more and more readers arose, and some had the Advertiser in them, and some had not. As American millionaires now appear to possess, with one or two exceptions, all the more priceless and perfect copies, I will deal with the best copy that I can get—and I am most grateful for the loan of it. In that copy the Pickwick Advertiser does not appear till the thirteenth number.

To the ordinary mortal who loves and knows his *Pickwick*, but is not a bibliophile or a collector, it is a truly romantic moment in which he first sees the immortal work in paper covers. The later books, however precious and fragile, cannot give quite the same thrill. Here in front of me as I write is the first number, bearing on the cover in a faded, elegant and illegible writing the name of its original owner, Mary Nunn of Epsom. Why did Miss Nunn buy it? Perhaps because she had read some of the *Sketches by Boz*, and thought them rather amusing, or perhaps just because she wanted something to read and liked the look of Seymour's pictures on the cover? We can imagine her growing more and more enthusiastic and more and more impatient as the time for each new number drew near, so that she stood outside the gate of her house at Epsom, and even wandered some way down the road looking for the boy who was to bring it from the bookseller. When at last he arrived she scolded him vehemently for being so late, accused him of having dallied on the road to look at it himself, tore it from him in a fury and then bolted herself into her own room to read it undisturbed.

There may be others as ignorant as I was, who have never seen *Pickwick* in its numbers. So I may say just a word about the cover. On the title page of any ordinary edition of *Pickwick* we read only, "The Posthumous Papers of the Pickwick Club," and personally I was so ignorant that I never knew before that there was any more. On the outside of the green numbers is the full title, "The Posthumous Papers of the Pickwick Club containing a faithful record of the Perambulations, Perils, Travels, Adventures and Sporting Transactions of the members." The "Sporting Transactions" have a special line and type all to themselves. We have often been told, of course, that Seymour's gift lay in the direction of Cockney sportsmen, that the Pickwick Club sprang from the suggestion of a Nimrod Club, that Dickens was originally engaged to write round Seymour's plates, and that he put in Mr. Winkle for the artist's especial benefit. Perhaps however we hardly realized how predominant the sporting element was intended to be until we looked at this cover. At the top is a thin gentleman in gaiters, of the Winkle type, firing point blank—from his left shoulder—at a large bird sitting on a small tree much as Mr. Winkle himself subsequently proposed to put a stuffed partridge on the top of a post and practise at it, beginning at a short distance. At the bottom is a stout gentleman in spectacles, presumably Mr. Pickwick, sitting in a punt which is moored in a river, with a church in the background. He has been fishing, but now the rod has dropped from his hand, and his head has dropped on his chest in slumber. A bottle and a pie dish suggest that he has been lunching, and two birds are finishing the pie. Whether it was ever intended that the Pickwickians should fish or whether Seymour simply

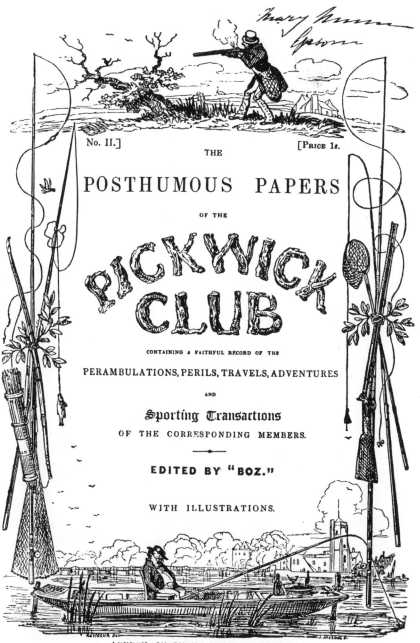

No. II.]

THE

POSTHUMOUS PAPERS

OF THE

PICKWICK CLUB

CONTAINING A FAITHFUL RECORD OF THE

PERAMBULATIONS, PERILS, TRAVELS, ADVENTURES

AND

Sporting Transactions

OF THE CORRESPONDING MEMBERS.

———

EDITED BY "BOZ."

WITH ILLUSTRATIONS.

[PRICE 1s.

LONDON: CHAPMAN & HALL, 186, STRAND.

MDCCCXXXVI.

drew what came easiest to him nobody can now tell. If they had fished, some of them would almost certainly have fallen into the water, and perhaps the skating scene took the place of the fishing one.

On either side of the page is a design of guns, rods, landing nets and so on entwined in a garland. Among them are a bow and a quiver full of arrows. So here is the foreshadowing of another adventure that never actually took place. If it had, no doubt, Mr. Winkle would have put an arrow into somebody. As it is the only arrows in the book were those carried in her quiver by Mrs. Pott when she went to Mrs. Leo Hunter's party as Apollo.

I have said elsewhere that the advertisers were, as a rule, very unenterprising as regards making use of Dickens characters, but that they did christen various of their goods after Mr. Pickwick. Of this there is evidence in the Pickwick Advertiser itself, for we find under the head of new music, composed by Boz Jun., the "Original Pickwick Quadrilles containing Pickwick, Winkle, Tupman, Snodgrass, Jingle and Sam Weller, nightly danced in the Royal and Almack Balls." This advertisement is subsequently repeated with the interesting addition of Princess Victoria's Birthday Quadrille and a "new National song" called "Victoria England's Daughter", the words by Alfred Conroy, and the music by "A Peer of the Realm." Was Alfred Conroy any connection of Sir John Conroy, the Duchess of Kent's confidential adviser and friend, whom Princess Victoria did not like, and Queen Victoria banished from her presence? I am afraid I do not know, but it would be tempting to invent a story that he was, and that he hoped to mollify the Princess toward Sir John by writing that song which has never, alas! become national.

The mention of Sir John Conroy must be allowed to tempt me for a moment from *Pickwick* to

Nickleby because in the seventeenth number of that work there is an interesting reverberation of the scandal which a little while before had broken out as to the unlucky Lady Flora Hastings. Jefferys & Co. of 31, Frith Street, Soho, had seen a chance of turning an honest penny out of it, and this is what the *Chronicle* said: "The decease of this highly accomplished, amiable and, we grieve to add, unfortunate lady, has called forth a Tributary Poem, in which we find so much of good feeling, united with the purest sentiment, that we have great pleasure in recommending it to the notice of all who feel interested in the cause of suffering innocence. The Poetry by Charles Jefferys has been beautifully set to Music by Nelson; and published, as it is, with a fine Portrait of Lady Flora Hastings cannot fail to become universally popular."

Generally speaking Pickwick wares, chintzes and canes and hats, do not appear in the Advertiser, but there is other evidence of the astonishing popularity which led to every kind of piracy and imitation, unauthorized adventures and endings and half a dozen plays and burlettas founded on the book. Artists conceived the notion of drawing their own pictures to the story and advertising them as being suitable to be bound up with the numbers in a book. There were "Pictures Picked from the Pickwick Papers by Alfred Crowquill, intended to illustrate a series of incidents from that popular work, which are too interesting to be lost sight of—differing in style and subject from those that have already appeared in the number." There were also, "Sam Weller's illustrations to the *Pickwick Papers* published by E. Grattan," as to which the *Chronicle* said, "In the first part Pickwick and Wardell [*sic*] are beyond praise; Sam Weller is a great hit, but his figure is too aristocratic; the whole group is admirably illustrative of the letter-press. In the last plate, Dr. Slammer and old

Pickwick are immense, the person to the left is the beau ideal of Dr. Cantwell in the play of 'The Hypocrite'; this plate is very fine. The artist must be a great man should he live; he has nothing of the caricature of George Cruickshank, which pervades all that artist's best performances; his pencil is more Hogarth-like and dramatical. Each figure is a study and the combinations are exquisitely good." We can not be greatly influenced by a critic who talks about "old Pickwick". It is as impossible as to talk of "old Woodhouse" in *Emma*; people who can do such things must be dead to all sense of shame. Incidentally the same sort of thing was done on a smaller scale to *Nickleby* as to *Pickwick*. Peter Palette advertised an additional set of illustrations to the book and there were also "Heads from Nicholas Nickleby. Etched by A. Drypoint." The drawings were attributed to Miss La Creevy, appropriately enough as she painted miniatures.

Another example of this tendency to pirate or copy *Pickwick* is a long advertisement headed "The Queer Fish Society", and purporting to report the Society's second special meeting at the Dog-in-Breeches tavern. It is an obvious and exceedingly poor imitation of the first chapter in *Pickwick* and the meeting of the Club. I will quote some of it as a curiosity. "As soon as the President had taken his seat it was announced by the Secretary, Mr. Jeremiah Pike, that a packet of papers had been delivered into his charge by Lieutenant Thunderem, which papers contained a series of notes concerning numerous surprising adventures in which the honourable and gallant officer had been engaged and which he wished to be perused by the President and the Committee for the purpose of their being arranged as a narrative. . . . It would appear that the veteran officer had, a few years ago, gone through great

D

dangers; that he had fallen in love and been most
shamefully jilted; that he had made a voyage to
foreign parts, in the course of which he would
have sunk to the bottom of the sea, had he not
contrived to swim ashore; and would have been
killed by a cannon ball, had it not missed him by
seven inches." And so on and on to an intoler-
able length. Mr. Scribble, "a literary gentleman,"
played the part of Mr. Blotton, of Aldgate, and
was duly crushed. The proceedings of the Society
were published under the name of *The Queer Fish
Chronicle*, in sixpenny numbers, by E. Steill, of
Paternoster Row.

All this Grub Street activity did not, of course,
begin any more than did the advertisements until
Pickwick became famous. So now perhaps it
would be best to go back to the beginning and
look at the advertisements such as they are on
the cover of the first number, before any question
of sewn-in sheets of a Pickwick Advertiser had
arisen. Here again there may be variations, and
I can only take them from the copy before me.
They were not intrinsically exciting, but they have
earned their niche just because they were the first
advertisements in the first number of *Pickwick*.
They are all of books and of books published by
the publishers of *Pickwick*, Chapman and Hall.

On the inside of the front cover there comes
first that "splendidly illustrated volume, *The Pictorial Album or Cabinet of Paintings for* 1837." It
contains eleven designs, executed in oils, "Colours
by G. Baxter and forming perfect facsimiles of the
original pictures." The poetry is by Miss Landon,
the prose by James Ollier, Esq., "the style of each
artist is imitated completely and the literature is
of high pretension and of an elevated nature."
Next comes *The Library of Fiction or Family Story
Teller*, "admirably adapted for fireside reading"
and having a distinguished list of contributors,

among them Boz, G. P. R. James, Miss Mitford,
Lady Blessington and Douglas Jerrold. It must
have been quite Podsnappishly suitable for family
reading, since the *Metropolitan Magazine* remarked
of it "There is not one that has contained aught
that might shock the purity of the most rigid
moralist or wound the feelings of the most serious
Christian." Equally suitable no doubt was the
Library's next door neighbour, *Edward the Crusader's
Son*, by Mrs. Barwell. It illustrated the manners
and customs of England in the eleventh century
and was intended for the use of "those instructors
who disapprove of the too stimulating pages of
historical romances."

On the inside of the back cover are some travelling and hunting maps, "The Artist or Young Ladies,
Instructor in Ornamental Painting, Drawing, etc."
and two anthologies, "A Garland of Love", which
is "wreathed of choice flowers gathered in the
Field of English Poetry," and "The Poetic Wreath".
In the second of these the pieces were arranged
alphabetically, and at the beginning of each letter
was "a beautiful device in wood engravings, repre-
senting that letter by a combination of cherubs."
On the outside three ladies, the aforesaid Mrs.
Barwell and Ann and M. M. Rodwell become
very active. Mrs. Barwell wrote "Remember, or
Mamma's Birthday," whereupon M. M. Rodwell
wrote "Caroline, or the Pleasures of a Birthday."
M. M. Rodwell also wrote "The Spoiled Child
Reclaimed," and the *Athenæum* said that the moral
lessons inculcated were "precisely those which it
is of most importance to impress on the youthful
mind." Ann Rodwell did not deal in morals, but
produced "The Juvenile Pianist, A Mirror of Music
for Infant Minds." Mrs. Barwell, not to be out-
done by all the Rodwells, then wrote "Nursery
Government, or Hints addressed to Mothers and
Nurserymaids," but her testimonial only came

from the *Salisbury Chronicle,* which was a poor
retort to the *Athenæum.* Amongst all those virtuous works is one much more dubious, a French
anthology called, "Fleurs de Poesie Moderne."

For a considerable time after this there is nothing
of much moment—merely the same books of
Chapman and Hall on the inside and outside cover.
The *Pictorial Album* points out that its pictures
are coloured, "nor is this additional fascination
wrought through the medium of mere water tints,"
but by "the richer and more enduring effects of
oil colours." The editor of the *Library of Fiction*
is very proud of completing his first volume and
adds, "We need scarcely enlarge upon the value
of such a publication. To the more desultory
reader, whose leisure or inclination does not suffice
for the perusal of elaborate works, yet who is by
no means indisposed to bask occasionally in the
sunlight of fancy and invention, it is more peculiarly
fitted; while as a companion to the family circle,
its persevering inculcation (though more by way
of indication than direct tutorage) of the purest
principles of morality will abundantly recommend
it."

No. XII is a landmark in that for the first time
we find on the cover advertisements of books published by another firm than Chapman and Hall,
and also of something that is not a book at all.
Messrs. Longman, Rees, Orme, Brown, Green and
Longman are the enterprising publishers and their
books include the famous Mr. G. P. R. James's
new romance, *Attila.* There are *Adventures in the
Moon and other worlds, Conversations on Mineralogy*
and *The Curate of Steinhollt,* a tale of Iceland in
two volumes; also *Fraser's Magazine,* containing
"The Diamond Necklace," by Thomas Carlyle.
The first advertisers to break through the ring of
publishers and booksellers are Cowen and Waring,
with their "newly invented Caoutchouc or India

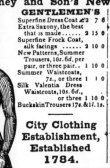

Rubber Canvas." They produce testimonials from three Royal Academicians, Reinagle, Westall and the great Constable himself, who says, "I must therefore consider the newly invented ground a great acquisition to the profession by rendering the labours of the artist secure."

And now at last with Number XIII in my set we come to the Pickwick Advertiser, which continues till the book was completed in the twentieth number. It is exceedingly fat and prosperous, and in Number XIV there is a note, "20,000 of the Advertising Sheet will be printed and stitched in each monthly number." I must take the advertisements in some form of classification, and by far the largest class is that including books or periodicals, but as we have already had some literature let us start with something else, and take Mr. Doudney the Tailor.

Mr. Doudney, who afterwards blossomed into Bond Street where NOBLEMEN were his customers, was at the moment in Lombard Street. He was a regular patron of the different Dickens advertisers, but in *Pickwick* he did what he never did afterwards, he wrote a poem. Possibly Mr. Moses afterwards seduced his poet, for there is a certain resemblance of style. Here are five verses of it.

How to get a Good Dressing

Reform the State, with voice elate let Politicians shout,
Reform the Lords, Reform the Church, Reform the Land throughout,
Reform your house, your plans, your purse, your ailments and your ills,
But oh! above all things, cry we, Reform Your Tailors' Bills.

Perhaps you say, in sore dismay, "How can the thing be done?"
Whereat we cry, Most easily with Doudney and Son,
Of Lombard Street at Forty nine, the number's on the door
Established anno seventeen hundred and eighty four.

Your person in a perfect suit they prominently fix,
In such as all who see admire for three pounds twelve and six;
Good work, good cloth, good quality and patterns all the go,
And morning coats, the price fifteen—the charge, you'll own
    is low.

And oh, ye Sportsmen, listen now while we your pleasures
    cater,
For two pounds ten your suit complete, including leathern
    gaiter.
Their trousers too of many sorts, for fishing or for trav'lling,
Their price is small—thirteen and six—and safe from all
    unrav'lling.

Moreover Doudneys were the first who very kindly proffered
Their yearly contracts for our clothes—-the cheapest ever
    offered.
Two suits a year at eight pounds six and three for twelve
    pounds five,
Or four for fifteen pounds eighteen—'Tis you the benefit derive.

That last line makes one doubt whether the
author was Mr. Moses's poet, for, if it was, he never
subsequently wrote one that scanned quite so out-
rageously ill.   Apart from his poem (and no other
advertiser wrote one in *Pickwick*) Mr. Doudney
was commonplace. So indeed were the sellers of
clothes as a whole, though it is pleasant to learn
that in a certain corset "Mrs. Geary's genius has
full swing," and that Mrs. G. was skilful in dealing
with "parts adapted to prominences."   I should
like to have seen the "new short-napped Beaver
hat," which had numerous unprincipled imitators,
but could only be bought from the original inventor,
Preedy of Fleet Street.   Attractive also in its way
was the "Pannus-Corium" or "Leather Cloth Shoe,"
which looked particularly well with a golosh worn
over it.
    Let us leave the clothiers and turn to the pill
and medicine men. There were several makers of
pills, but by far the greatest of them, Morison,
was still climbing the lower rungs and had little

to say for himself. There were Cockle's Antibilious
pills, "prepared by Mr. James Cockle, Surgeon
Extraordinary to Her Serene Highness the Land-
gravine of Hesse Homberg." There were Dr. John
Armstrong's Liver Pills, "scientifically prepared for
the proprietor, a gentleman of private fortune."
There were Norton's Camomile Pills—quite dull—
and the Antibilious ones of Mr. Simpson. He also
made "Herbal Remedies" and "Young persons,
wasting away and with every appearance of going
into a decline by taking two or three boxes have
been entirely cured." The only one to soar at all
beyond the ordinary was Dr. Brandreth, a most
disarming and ingenuous person. "It matters not,"
he remarked, "what Mr. Morison or Dr. Brandreth
say about their Pills of Vegetable, but what
medicine is really the best. That Brandreth's
Pills are the most direct Purifiers there can be no
doubt." The reason why they were the best
was apparently that they obtained their sales
without advertising.

"Mineral Magnets" were a rather mysterious
remedy invented by Dr. Schmidt of Berlin, who,
"Having discovered a method of constructing magnets of any power of attraction, has succeeded in
establishing their use as a certain and powerful
remedy when applied, according to his own practice, to"—apparently almost any known complaint.
The Doctor lived in Half Moon Street, where he could
be consulted. I am not sure whether he could attract
away corns by his magnets, but there was another
rather amusing gentleman who could cure them.
"In the neighbourhood of Mark Lane, Corns of
various kinds fluctuate from day to day and
naturally create equal excitement amongst both
buyers and sellers. But there are Corns of another
description which create a still greater and more
painful excitement amongst both large and small
holders," and so on. The "Patent Self-tooth-filler"

leaves a good deal to the imagination whereas the picture of the lady curing her toothache is much more explicit. She is apparently smoking a long tube which passes through two urns. Thus she is obtaining "fumigation and steam from foreign herbs" which destroys the nerve without pain in three seconds. In appearance she is not unlike a lady in *Nickleby* who was cured by Beaufoy's

The Pickwick Advertiser

TOOTH-ACHE.

MR. LOCK continues to CURE the TOOTH-ACHE by fumigation or steam from foreign herbs, which has the effect of destroying the nerve without causing any pain to the patient. The cure is effected in three seconds, the tooth remains firm in the socket, and will not decay any further. The patient will, after this operation, be able to draw into the mouth the external air, strike the teeth together, or hold cold water in the mouth, without any pain. The advertiser has a tooth cured 15 years, therefore he can warrant the cure this length of time.—362, Oxford-street, three doors below the Pantheon. Letters post paid. Reference given if required. Charges moderate, according to the circumstances of the patients. This method is not injurious to the health or teeth.

instant Cure for the Toothache. "O! my dear Mrs. Goodbody," that lady is saying to her neighbour, "I am distracted with the Tooth Ache," and the neighbour, who comes prancing into the room with offensive cheerfulness, replies, "Well, love! I have brought you something that will cure it in an instant."

Under the same medicinal heading may come the advertisement of one of the last of the healing

wells or springs in which London was once rich,
the "Royal Beulah Spa and Garden, Norwood."
Indeed the Beulah Spa Hotel is still there to-day,
though Norwood is not so rustic as when Mr.
Spenlow had his country house there and David
Copperfield stayed with him for the week-end to
fall into hopeless captivity before Dora. This Spa
had "saline water eminently beneficial in all those
diseases in which the most celebrated mineral
aperient Springs have been found to afford relief."
It had also a military band, a space for archery
and another set aside for picnic parties. "The
delightful and romantic grounds have undergone
continued improvements, and to those whom a day
of tranquil enjoyment and unexceptional relaxa-
tion is desirable the advantages of Beulah Spa may
be confidently proffered as combining every induce-
ment that can be yielded by invigorating air,
delightful prospects and the efforts of Art to embel-
lish the charm of nature."

The hair-oil merchants headed by the venerable
and illustrious Rowland were reasonably active in
the Pickwickian era, whereas soap was just soap:
mankind presumably went into a shop and asked
for it, without troubling to inquire who made it.
In this regard however I owe an apology. I have
said earlier that Pears was the first of the soap
men and that he did not appear and then only
in a mild form till the time of *Edwin Drood*. There
was one long before him. Here in *Pickwick* is Mr.
Pittis of the Isle of Wight who advertises his
Arenean Soap. It is "the result of Chemical and
Geological research in the Isle of Wight, among
whose enchanting cliffs a substance has recently
been discovered possessing qualities of a saponaceous
character." Mr. Pittis appears only once whereas
Rowland is constant but has not yet by any means
risen to his full heights of eloquence. He proclaims
regularly his Kalydor, his Odonto and pearl dentifrice

and his Macassar oil which "preserves the hair
in curl and other decorative formation." To rhyme
with Rowland there is Mr. Gowland with his
"Lotions," there is also Ede, maker of the Odori-
ferous Compound or Persian Sweet bag, which
reminds me somehow of the Madagascar Liquid
about which Miss Mowcher talked to Steerforth and
David Copperfield. Much the most picturesque
however, is Mr. Oldridge, who makes Oldridge's
Balm and has a really beautiful picture of a lady

BRITISH CONSUL'S OFFICE,
Philadelphia.—Know all Persons to whom these
presents shall come, that I, Gilbert Robertson, Esq.,
his Britannic Majesty's Consul, do hereby certify, that
R. Warton, Esq. (who attests to the efficacy of OLD-
RIDGE'S BALM of COLUMBIA in RESTORING
HAIR), is Mayor of this City, and that M. Randall,
Esq., is Prothonotary of the Court of Common Pleas,
to both whose signatures full faith and credit is due.
I further certify that I am personally acquainted with
J. L. Inglis, Esq., another of the signers, and that he
is a person of great respectability, and that I heard
him express his unqualified approbation of the effects
of Oldridge's Balm in restoring his Hair.   Given under my hand and seal of office, at the City of Philadelphia, Dec.
29, 1823.   (Signed)   GILBERT ROBERTSON.
   Oldridge's Balm causes Whiskers and Eyebrows to grow, prevents the Hair from turning grey, and the first application makes it curl beautifully, frees it from scurf, and stops it from falling off. Abundance of Certificates from
gentlemen of the first respectability in England are shown by the Proprietors, C. and A. OLDRIDGE, 1, Wellington-
street, Strand, where the Balm is sold, and by all respectable Perfumers and Medicine Venders. Price 3s. 6d., 6s.
and 11s. per Bottle. No other prices are genuine.
   N.B. The Public are requested to be on their guard against Counterfeits. Ask for OLDRIDGE'S BALM, 1,
Wellington Street, Strand.

naked to the waist, with leopard-skin knicker-
bockers and a bow and arrow, against a background of river, ships and palm trees. Next door
to this picture is a solemn certificate given by the
British Consul in Philadelphia that "R. Warton
who attests the efficacy of Oldridge's Balm is Mayor
of this city, and that M. Randall, Esq., is Prothonotary of the Court of Common Pleas, to both of
whose signatures full faith and credit is due." As
to who this lady is in the picture I have no clue.
   There are one or two musical advertisements.
"W. and N. Boag solicit the attention of Flute Players
to an extensive collection of flutes," and in the same

number is "The Seraphine or Portable Organ, now brought to the greatest perfection, the beauties of which are not to be equalled for sweetness of tone, coupled with extraordinary power, although in size not larger than a Cheffonier." A set of comic songs have rather agreeable names. "The Rail Road," "Quang Chi and Fum Ho, or Love in China," "I'm quite a ladies' man," "The Islington Tailor and his Steam Goose" and "That's the way the money goes." Travelling by train was no doubt new enough for its discomforts to be exquisitely amusing in themselves, just as later the telegram was enough to supply the chief incident in a well known farce. "I'm quite a ladies' man" was sung of course by a gentleman with an opera hat and a shiny shirt front, and "That's the way the money goes" is presumably "Pop goes the Weazle," but as to the "Tailor and the Steam Goose," I cannot hazard a guess. Musicians were also incited to buy a portrait of the famous Malibran one-eighth of an inch by half an inch. The *Brixton Gazette* said "A more beautiful fairy-like production we have never seen" and the *Weekly True Sun* said it "would set in a ring." I know a lady who in her youth used to wear Henry Neville in a locket: so perhaps young gentlemen wore Madame Malibran in a ring.

The book advertisements are voluminous, and a good many of them are quite dull and show no enterprise. Lockhart's *Life of Scott* occupies no less than sixteen closely printed pages of tiniest type in the eighteenth number, but it is difficult to believe that many readers were thereby attracted to that great work. There are indexes to the different volumes and the contents of various chapters almost needing a microscope, and then page after page of the comments of newspapers and periodicals carefully arranged in alphabetical order.

The number of annuals and miscellanies and picture books is astonishing. There is the *Pictorial Album* before mentioned, and there is the *Keepsake*. The name will be familiar to those who know their *Middlemarch*. Mr. Ned Plymdale, Rosamond's well-to-do admirer, had brought with him to dinner at the Vincys "the last *Keepsake*, the gorgeous watered-silk publication which marked modern progress at that time; and he considered himself very fortunate that he could be the first to look over it with her, dwelling on the ladies and gentlemen with shiny copper-plate cheeks and copper-plate smiles, and pointing to comic verses as capital and sentimental stories as interesting." Rosamond was being very gracious, and Mr. Plymdale thought he was making progress, and then in came that odious rude prig of a Lydgate, who laughed scornfully at the *Keepsake*, and said he wondered which would be the silliest, the engravings or the writings —and poor Mr. Ned's castle in the air was shattered.

Much the same as the *Keepsake* was the *Book of Beauty*, and there were also *Gems of Beauty*, among which was displayed "a series of twelve highly finished engravings of the Passions" with verses by the Countess of Blessington. There was a book of Seymour's Sketches, to be carried to success on the tide of *Pickwick's* popularity; the publishers made the most of the "drawings of delightful Mr. Pickwick and the other characters of the Pickwick Club, they being originally designed by this Prince of Humourists, who is now no more and we may never see the like again." Tom Hood edited for A. H. Baily the *Comic Annual* of 1838, and wrote him a letter in his best style saying that he could not possibly publish the annual in November, so near the publication of "that splendid annual The Lord Mayor of London." He goes on "I think I told you that I had picked up some little German whims and oddities during a halt by

No. I. will appear on the 4th of May, Price 2d.

ADDRESS.

THE WASP is a general stinger;—but our WASP is a young gentleman who will exercise that function with a vast deal of discretion, stinging only those Excrescences in the Political and Fashionable World that from the obliquity of their conduct are deserving of a little wholesome chastisement. This will be administered very fearlessly, but in a very gentlemanly manner, so that, on all occasions, punishment and politeness shall go hand in hand.

Until the establishment of " The John Bull "—" The Age "—and " The Satirist," both men and things were not called by their right names. " The Bull " was the first to *kick* off the mask of imposture, behind which many Political and Titled Charlatans sheltered themselves; " The Age " did the same for the Fashionable World; and left it to " The Satirist " to produce a scourge compounded from the chastising rods of this bitter brace of predecessors. Something still remains to be done in the same line, there is just room left for a neat little stinger like " THE WASP " to fly in between them;—we mean him to come out on the mid-day of the week, and to be full of Novelty—Fun—Satire—and Whimsical Vivacity—for the low price of Two Pence ! Our Politics are of the most liberal kind, without being too Democratic. We like good and cheap Government, have a proper respect for the Kingly Prerogative, and a great regard for the Liberties of the People: these opinions we shall support on all occasions with the most uncompromising ardour and fidelity.

Regarding that ambiguous phrase, " Criticism," whether in Literature—the Fine Arts—or the Drama, we beg to say, we are knowing fellows, and understand the whole machinery of it, and will expose this monstrosity of humbug whenever we have an opportunity. The Public—that innocent, unsuspecting lamb—shall not be kidnapped into the admiration of Trumpery,

from seeing it lauded in the imperishable columns of " THE WASP." Every *buttering-up* criticism we read in the pages of our contemporaries, we can tell at a glance the number of dinners that have been demolished to produce it. Authors in general are a poor set, and cannot well bribe the Newspaper Critics, but then their sleek-headed Publishers are invariably wealthy, and can do it for them—so the business is thus managed very comfortably for all Parties.

The Stage is in an equally hopeful way—Actors can now play Macbeth—Mungo—or Massaniello,—and be admired in print from one glass of brandy-and-water to a gallon, the eulogy proceeding progressively with the given quantity of liquor. All this beautifully dove-tailed imposture we shall endeavour to *squabash* with our Literary Tomahawks. We give fair warning—we have ordered a score of scalping knives, and we are going to work in right earnest.

To be serious and to conclude;—Genius, Talent, and Public Virtue and Patriotism will always find an able advocate in " The Wasp." It is only with the Impostors of the Day that we wage an exterminating conflict, and to them we re-echo the celebrated Spanish Battle Cry of " War to the Knife."

" THE WASP " will appear (illustrated with two woodcuts, ably sketched by Rigdum Funnidos)—when Wasps generally do appear—in the genial and " merry month of May."—On Thursday, the 4th, the Public may look out for him, on the Counter of our Publisher, E. GRATTAN, 51, Paternoster Row, St. Paul's; and at every Newsvender's throughout the Metropolis.

N.B. Booksellers, Newsmen, &c. may procure a Dozen or more of this Work, with liberal Allowance, on Sale or Return.

the Rhine and a march with a Prussian regiment.
They are in a fair way to getting on box-wood
and into paper and print; and you may therefore
add them to my list of irons in the fire. N.B. or
Nota Baily, the fire is not only laid but lighted;
in witness thereof I send you some of the sticks,
that is to say, blocks.''

Ward's Miscellany has an entertaining announcement, in which the publishers are afraid that their
too lively prospectus has given a wrong impression
to the more serious among their potential readers.
''The vivacity with which it was written, while it
treated of the gravest subjects and promised that
the work it was to introduce should be consecrated
to the highest and holiest purpose, operated, we
have reason to fear, to its disadvantage among a
certain class of readers. By some it was under-
stood literally, and of course sneered at as a mag-
niloquent attempt to out-puff all the puffers, who
had rendered themselves victorious in this puffing
generation. Those who viewed it as mere irony,
written with the exclusive design of laughing at
the gross abuse of public confidence which had
excited towards prospectuses in general such almost
universal derision and contempt, censured its
arrogance.'' Nobody, it seems, could believe in
this unlucky prospectus because nobody could
believe it possible, ''to write things totally incom-
patible and to propitiate tastes and principles as
widely apart from one another as the poles.'' At
any rate the publishers did their best in this respect,
for among the contents were ''Divine Condescen-
sion,'' ''The Salmon Fisher,'' ''Eastern Abomina-
tions'' and ''Maiden Aunts.''

A really stimulating and appetizing prospectus is
that of *The Wasp* a new periodical intended, as
one supposes, to sail as near the wind as possible
in the matter of scandalous gossip, blackmail and
the law of libel. ''The Wasp is a general stinger

E

but our Wasp is a young gentleman who will exercise that function with a vast deal of discretion, stinging only those excrescences in the Political and Fashionable world that from the obliquity of their conduct are deserving of a little wholesome chastisement. This will be administered very fearlessly but in a very gentlemanly manner, so that on all occasions, punishment and politeness shall go hand in hand. . . . Regarding the ambiguous phrase "Criticism" whether in Literature, the Fine Arts or the Drama, we beg to say we are knowing fellows and understand the whole machinery of it, and will expose that monstrosity of humbug whenever we have an opportunity. The Public—that innocent, unsuspecting lamb—shall not be kidnapped into the admiration of Trumpery from seeing it lauded in the imperishable columns of "The Wasp." Every buttering-up criticism we read in the pages of our contemporaries we can tell at a glance the number of dinners that have been demolished to produce it. Authors in general are a poor set and cannot well bribe the newspaper critics, but then their sleek-headed publishers are invariably wealthy and can do it for them. So the business is thus managed very comfortably for all parties. The Stage is in an equally hopeful way. Actors can now play Macbeth, Mungo or Massaniello and be admired in print from one glass of brandy and water to a gallon, the Eulogy proceeding progressively with the given quantity of liquid. All this beautiful dove-tailed imposture we shall endeavour to *squabash* with our Literary Tomahawk. We give fair warning. We have ordered a score of scalping knives and we are going to work in right earnest." Let us hope they got at least a glass of brandy and water or two out of the sleek-headed publishers.

The annuals and keepsakes were for the comparatively emancipated. They would not do for the

genuine "Young Person". Several works suitable to
her have already been specified, but nobody produced
so many or such eminently safe ones as a certain
Mrs. Hofland. They were called "Juvenile or Prize
Books" and she wrote one on nearly every one
of the Christian virtues. There were Decision,
Energy, Fortitude, Humility, Integrity, Modera-
tion, Patience, Reflection, Self Denial. Each was
called "A tale" and cost five shillings. She further
wrote *The Affectionate Brother, Alice and her Aunts,
The Merchant's Widow, or her Young Family* and
Rich Boys and Poor Boys. No one else was so pro-
lific but I would willingly give up all her works
for a sight of *Morals from the Church Yard.
A Series of Cheerful Tales for Youth of Both
Sexes.*

Amongst the more miscellaneous books that
sound attractive is *Hints on Etiquette, or the Usages
of Society,* published by Longmans and, according
to the *Domestic Magazine,* "Equally necessary to
the most elevated and most ordinary mind, and
not less to the man of principle and piety than
to the man of the world." So does *The Golden
Rules of Life* which "contain the maxims and
Rules of some hundred great and good men who
lived to be Benefactors to their Country, collected
from upwards of a thousand works." Both the
title and the nature of the work suggest that the
author anticipated Sir John Lubbock.

Equally agreeable and romantic into the bargain
are the remarks of Edward William Lane Esquire
about his new translations of the *Arabian Nights.*
He knows all about the Arabs and has "resided
in a land where genii are still firmly believed to
obey the summons of the magician or the owner
of a talisman and to act in occurrences of every
day, and he has listened to stories of their deeds
related by persons of the highest respectability
and by some who would not condescend to read

the Tales of 1001 Nights merely because they are
fictitious."

Now one or two miscellaneous advertisers
deserve a word, particularly our old friend Madame
Tussaud. The figures specifically mentioned are
nearly all royalties and there is not a word of the
Chamber of Horrors unless the "Second Room",
for which an additional 6*d*. is charged, is an
euphemistic name for it. Here is the announcement: "Her Majesty Victoria the First, Her
August Mother the Duchess of Kent, His late
Majesty King William IV, the Dowager Queen
Adelaide, the King of Hanover, the Duke of Sussex
and the Duke of Wellington, with all the leading
characters of the day—the whole taken from life,
are now added to Madame Tussaud & Sons' Exhibition and Bazaar, Baker Street, Portman Square.
Admittance 1*s*., Second Room 6*d*. Open 11—6
and 7—10. Brilliantly illuminated." One can not
help feeling that a murderer or two would have
added a cheerful note.

"It is a sin to steal a pin", but the precise kind
of pin is not generally supposed to affect the question. However there was in 1837 a very particular
kind of pin, "the splendid new pin with immov-
able solid head, patronised by Her Majesty and all
the Royal Princesses," and possessing "a brilliant
silver-like appearance and incomparable points."
With this we may compare the "Ne plus ultra
pin" with "perfect solid head and smooth adamantine point." It was a British pin, and British also
were the "Home-made Macaroni and Vermicelli",
but it appears that unpatriotic persons would not
buy them because they ought to have come from
Italy. "It has always," said the makers, "appeared
to us anomalous that Englishmen, while universally
prefering to admire and uphold the institutions,
fame and character of their own country, almost
as universally evince a strong partiality for articles

IMPORTANT TO LADIES.

FAILURE TO OBTAIN   **AN INJUNCTION**

TO RESTRAIN THE   MANUFACTURE OF

NE PLUS ULTRA PINS,
With perfect Solid Heads and smooth Adamantine Points.

RESULT OF LITIGATION.

A COPY OF A NOTICE served on Messrs. KIRBY, BEARD, and Co., dated the 31st of December, 1840, and signed, "White and Borrett," solicitors to the Assignees of Henry Shuttleworth, a bankrupt, and circulated in a letter, signed "J. Briggs, for D. F. Tayler and Co.," dated the 1st of January, 1841, having been sent to several of the customers of Kirby, Beard, and Co., and re-issued more recently, to the effect, that "Any persons purchasing or vending Solid Headed Pins in violation of the alleged Patent rights of such Assignees, were liable to be called to account like any other PIRATES." Messrs. KIRBY, BEARD, and Co. think it right to communicate to their customers and consumers of Pins, the result of the litigation which has taken place in the Courts of Chancery and Queen's Bench, between MARLING and OTHERS, as assignees of the said HENRY SHUTTLEWORTH, and KIRBY, BEARD, and Co.

"MARLING and KIRBY, RE SHUTTLEWORTH.

"It is mutually agreed between the assignees of Mr. Henry Shuttleworth, and Messrs. Kirby, Beard, and Co., that the assignees shall withdraw all their proceedings against Messrs. Kirby, Beard, and Co. relating to 'Wright's Patent,' for making Solid Headed Pins, and that the assignees shall pay TWO HUNDRED AND TWENTY-FIVE POUNDS in discharge of the costs of Messrs. Kirby, Beard, and Co. Dated this 10th day of December, 1842.

(Signed)

WHITE and BORRETT, *Solicitors for and on the behalf of the Assignees of Henry Shuttleworth.*
HUGHES, KEARSEY, and MASTERMAN, *Solicitors for and on behalf of Kirby, Beard, and Co."*

KIRBY, BEARD, and Co., Pin and Needle Makers to Her Most Excellent Majesty Queen Victoria and the Dowager Queen Adelaide, with a grateful recollection of many years' distinguished and extensive public patronage, preference, and support, respectfully solicit the attention of their Customers and Consumers of Pins and Needles to their HIGHEST QUALITY OF PINS, known from all other Pins in the Trade, by the name of "KIRBY'S NE PLUS ULTRA PINS, WITH PERFECT SOLID HEADS AND SMOOTH ADAMANTINE POINTS"—the product, at a great expence, of many years' experiments and improvement upon the *original invention* and *first patent taken out* for the manufacture of Solid Headed Pins. An eminent Engineer, on an inspection of KIRBY, BEARD, and Co.'s New Machinery in daily operation, described it —"*As combining the skilful application of the most ingenious mechanism, practically applied in its minutest construction and operations to effect uniformly the highest quality and finish to Pins with Solid Heads.*" Notwithstanding the above quite original and true description printed on the labels and wrapers of KIRBY, BEARD, and Co.'s Pins, the same has been and is dexterously copied and counterfeited, with the omission of the words "*Kirby's*" and "*Smooth,*" by a firm of Solid Headed Pin Makers, *untruly* calling themselves *exclusive* patentees, who, by such piracy and in a spirit of great unfairness as tradesmen one towards another, advertise and sell, by such description, their Solid Headed Pins of a SECOND PRICE, and consequently of a SECOND AND INFERIOR QUALITY.

The attention of the public and consumers being thus directed to this species of deception, and the perverted application of the words " NE PLUS ULTRA " against their obvious sense and meaning, they will readily distinguish the ORIGINAL AND GENUINE ARTICLE from the RECENT COUNTERFEIT; and Ladies, should they wish to purchase the former, are respectfully solicited (to prevent mistakes) to ask for KIRBY'S NE PLUS ULTRA PINS," which, as well as

EMBOSSED LABEL.

NE PLUS ULTRA NEEDLES,
With perfect Drilled Eyes,

For the convenience of purchasers (as well as in the usual manner), *Kirby and Co.* make up their *Ne Plus Ultra Needles* in a variety of Medallion Cases, each containing One Hundred of assorted useful sizes; also in *Morocco, Rich Satin, and Superb Velvet Cases,* containing Ten Papers of useful sorts and sizes, which includes One Paper of all the unique and best adapted *perfect Needles,* expressly manufactured for every description of modern and elegant *Ladies' Fancy Needle Work.* Also, their *Kirby's Ne Plus Ultra Pins,* in superb Cases, containing Six Papers of the most approved sizes, forming useful appendages to a Ladies' Repository, a choice of *these elegant little Presents* are sold at *very moderate prices* at all the leading Haberdashers, Silk Mercers, and Linen Drapers in the United Kingdom, and every part of Europe and America.——Every description of Pins, Needles, and Fish Hooks to be had, Wholesale and for Exportation, at KIRBY, BEARD, and Co.'s Manufactories.

No. 46, Cannon Street, London, and Gloucester.

of foreign production not on account of any superiority they possess over the productions of their own country but merely because they are foreign."

Patent pedometers for pedestrians to wear in the waistcoat pocket sound agreeably mysterious, but much more so is the sound of two racecourses, one for steeplechases and one for flat-races, in the Bayswater Road close to the Park. "The Hippodrome of Bayswater near Hyde Park within five hundred yards of the walls of Kensington Gardens, consists of a Park of considerable extent, the circumference being upwards of two miles, surrounded by a high strong paling and containing two racecourses. The First of these is in a rough state intersected by brooks and every description of fence and adapted for races similar to steeple chases. The second is a regular racecourse which will at all seasons be preserved in the finest order and be suited to races of the first class. In the centre of the park is a hill railed in from which a full view is enjoyed by pedestrians." It is further stated that ladies and children can ride there, and hunters be trained, and that there will be no gambling booths and no drink.

It sounds like a dream, but it was sober fact and can be read about in *Old and New London*. Its fame did not last, and the site is long since blotted out, but here is what the *Sporting Magazine* of 1837 said about it. "Making the *cours aristocratique* of Routine (alias Rotten) Row, you pass out at Cumberland Gate, and then trot on to Bayswater. Thence you arrive at the Kensington Gravel Pits and, descending where on the left stands the terrace of Notting Hill, find yourself opposite the large wooden gates of a recent structure. Entering there, I was by no means prepared for what opened upon me. Here, without figure of speech, was the most perfect race-course that I had ever seen. Conceive, almost within the bills of mortality, an enclosure

some two and half miles in circuit, commanding
from its centre a view as spacious and enchanting
as that from Richmond Hill (?) and where almost
the only thing you can *not* see is London.   Around
this, on the extreme circle, next to the lofty fence
by which it is protected . . . is constructed or
rather laid out—for the leaps are natural fences—
the steeplechase course of two miles and a quarter.
Within this, divided by a slight trench, and from
the space appropriated to carriages and equestrians
by strong and handsome posts all the way round,
is the racecourse, less probably than a furlong in
circuit.   Then comes the enclosure for those who
ride or drive as aforesaid; and lastly, the middle,
occupied by a hill, from which every yard of the
running is commanded, besides miles of country
on every side beyond it, and exclusively reserved
for foot people."

The *Racing Calendar* for 1837 mentions two races
run in the Hippodrome for £50 and £100 respectively.   The actual opening was on the 3rd June
in that year, there was a brilliant assembly, and
the stewards were the great Count D'Orsay and
Lord Chesterfield.   Yet it petered out in 1841, and
the reason as given in *Rural Sports* was "Unfortunately the proprietors overlooked one circumstance
at once fatal to the Hippodrome; the soil was a
deep, strong clay, so that the training-ground could
be used by horses only at particular periods of the
year.   This was a difficulty not to be got over
and as a race-course the Hippodrome soon closed
its short career, doubtless with a heavy loss to the
proprietors."   Some of the turf and the hedges
remained, "over which dashing young ladies would
ride their chargers as lately as the year 1852."
There seems in this forgotten London racecourse
the material for another unrecorded adventure of
Mr. Winkle's.

CHAPTER IV

THE YOUNG PERSON

"HE trusts that, throughout this book, no
incident or expression occurs which could
call a blush into the most delicate cheek or wound
the feelings of the most sensitive person." So
wrote Dickens in his preface to *Pickwick*. I wonder
if he recalled the words with just the suspicion of
a blush when years afterwards he put words not
unlike them into the mouth of Mr. Podsnap, the

---

patron saint of the young person. Mr. Podsnap
believed the young person to be embodied in his
daughter Georgiana, and "the question about everything was, would it bring a blush into the cheek
of the young person." A great many things did
so, especially things which came from countries
that had the misfortune to be foreign. "And if
we were all Englishmen present I would say,"

added Mr. Podsnap, "that there is in the Englishman a combination of qualities, a modesty, an
independence, a responsibility, a repose, combined
with an absence of everything calculated to call
a blush into the cheek of the young person, which
one would seek in vain among the Nations of the
Earth."

Therefore when we look at the advertisements
of books or games or amusements intended for the
edification of the young person we think naturally
of Mr. Podsnap acting as a censor before Georgiana

---

might look at them. Poor Georgiana was so
crushed by the "awfulness" of her papa and mamma
and indeed of everybody else that it is hard to
know what she would have liked if she had been
allowed. The only half-formed wish that she
cherished was that of having been born a chimney
sweep on May-day. Then she might have liked
dancing: as it was she didn't like it nor music nor
talking: reading "she didn't mind so much", and
so as we set out to find something for her in these
advertisements we have few clues to her tastes.

Would she for instance, have liked, *Home Influence, a Tale for Mothers and Daughters?* It was strongly recommended by the newspapers, one of which remarked "There are some very charming people in these volumes, about whom it is really delightful to read. Mrs. Hamilton is quite a model to mothers—so sensible and yet so gentle—so serene in her wisdom, and so strict in principle and yet so tolerant in practice." *The Indian News* said that if placed in children's hands it would be "a monitor which might hereafter be not without its effect." Then there was *The Holy Homes*—a tale by Silverpen, and there was always *The Family Herald,* for amusing reading "such as may be admitted to one's household without fear of consequences." Equally safe was *The Young Englishwoman,* a magazine which might "be placed without the slightest fear in the hands of girls of tender age." I am sure Mr. Podsnap would have thought all of them eminently suitable works; but unfortunately the publishers, while giving prominence to these admirable books, did not exercise sufficient care in some of their other advertisements, for cheek by jowl with *The Holy Homes* was a book called *The Cannibal Crusoe.* It was this kind of book which so utterly failed to promote moral thoughtfulness. Dr. Arnold had strongly disapproved of them. "Childishness in boys," he once wrote in a letter to a serious friend, "even of good abilities, seems to me to be a growing fault, and I do not know to what to ascribe it, except to the great number of exciting books of amusement like *Pickwick* or *Nickleby.*" The same objections would certainly apply to Mayne Reid, whose book called *The Headless Horseman* was actually advertised in Mr. Podsnap's very own book, *Our Mutual Friend.* There was a perfectly disgraceful picture of an Indian brave sitting on his horse and actually without a head.

Then there were other books which while not positively harmful were yet, as their very names indicated, silly and frivolous to a degree. Here are some of them taken from a number of *Bleak House :* Funny Leaves for the Younger Branches by the Baron Krakensides, Tales from Catland, written for Little Kittens by an old Tabby, A Choice Collection of Riddles, Charades, Conundrums, Parlour Games and Forfeits by Peter Puzzlewell, Esq. Mr. Podsnap would have thought himself a reasonable man; he would not have gone quite so far as Mr. Gradgrind, who wanted children taught nothing but facts. He would have allowed something beside Dr. Mantell's Lectures on the Wonders of Geology: (and by the way since these were advertised in *Nickleby* why did not the Doctor call himself Mantalini?) He really could not, however, have approved of conundrums and riddles; you never could tell when the most innocent-looking riddle would have a double meaning eminently calculated to bring the blush.

Worse however than any of these things were the songs to be found in Jullien's Album, which had four whole pages devoted to it in the Dombey Advertiser. The prospectus on the first page appeared respectable enough. It certainly was a pity, as Mr. Podsnap thought, that among the contributors were a number of foreigners having such outlandish names as Verdi and Donizetti, but the allusion to "numerous influential patrons" was reassuring and made Mr. Podsnap pull up his shirt collar and assume in advance an air of beneficent patronage. When, however, he turned over the page and looked at some of the extracts, he could hardly believe his eyes. Here was a song called "The First Lesson" composed by Balfe with words by a person of the name of Bayley. It was so outrageous, so calculated to put ideas into a young person's head and make her heart feel prematurely

A MAIDEN SOUGHT THE DEWY GROVE.

Composed by HŒLZEL.
Written by J. W. MOULD.

A maiden sought the dewy grove,
  When morn woke earth to joy;
Her recent path, there then pursued ·
  A brave young hunter boy.

When in the grove, the youth enquir'd
  "Sweet maid, what dost thou there ?"
She answered straight, " to gather wood
  I to the wood repair."

He said, " ah let the branch uncull'd
  Beside its parent lie;
Come ! I would taste thy ruby lip,
  And smile into thine eye."

" Go, leave me !" cried the laughing maid
  "These eyes are liquid blue,
The hunter's badge is green or grey,
  Then green grey eyes for you !"

" O cunning scholar," answer'd he,
  Your reas'ning holds not true,
Dost see where now yon bird I shoot,
  . Is not that heaven blue?

" But let me win thy dainty kiss,
  And laugh into these eyes ;
They, too. afford a heav'nly bliss,
  A nearer paradise."

" Then kiss and smile, if both thou wilt,
  But kiss and smile with truth ;
Nor darken with Dishonor's cloud,
  The pure bright heav'n of youth."

ROSALIE.

Composed by A. M. R. BARRET.
Written by J. W. LAKE.

Forget thee! no, my Rosalie,
  I never can forget
Those hours so sweet to memory,
  When we were children yet.
When hand and heart together wove,
  Beneath the greenwood tree,
We lov'd unknowing what was love,
  My charming Rosalie.
When hand and heart together wove, &c.

Forget thee! no, my Rosalie,
  'Tis not my faith to prove;
Thou mak'st this fond reproach to me.
  'Tis but a wile of love !
Thy woman's heart such doubt disowns,
  Thou know'st it cannot be;
I would not for a thousand thrones
  Forget thee ! no, my Rosalie !

WHEN THE HEART IS FOND AND TRUE !

Composed by A. M. R. BARRET.
Written by J. HURRY.

When the heart is fond and true,
  Sweetly, time is flying;
When your lover comes to woo,
  Gaily, fondly sighing;
Vows of promise charm the soul,
  Joy will dance before ye ;
And the god of love well pleased,
  Will keep watching o'er ye.
When the heart is fond and true, &c.

Then life's full of golden dreams,
  Free from care and sorrow;
And the heart, from future scenes,
  Sunny hopes will borrow !
Earth will like a heaven be,
  Full of joy and gladness ;
And the world will seem to bear
  Not a shade of sadness !

When the heart is fond and true,
  Sweetly time is flying ;
When your lover comes to woo.
  Gaily, fondly sighing;
Thoughts of bliss will charm the soul,
  Hope shine bright before ye;
And Heav'n itself will seem to smile
  In approbation o'er ye !

NAY, SMILE AGAIN !*

Arranged by H. FARMER.
Written by J. L. FORREST.

Nay smile again ! 'tis joy to me
  To gaze on that fair open brow,
And mark the silent witchery
  That breathes so sweetly round it now.
That smile again ! its sparkling grace
  Recalls bright thoughts of happier years,
Ere grief had dimm'd that joyous face,
  Or fill'd those soft blue eyes with tears.
Nay smile again, 'tis joy to me, &c.

Then smile again ! such glorious light
  Is shed around that placid face,
When sadness wings her sullen flight,
  And joy sits thron'd in beaming grace.
But smile again ! Oh, smile again !
  For ere the passing radiance flies
My soul would gaze, and gazing fain
  Find Heav'n within those lustrous eyes !
Nay smile again ! 'tis joy to me, &c.

* The melody of this beautiful Ballad is taken from Jullien's celebrated Bridal Waltz.

conscious of a vacancy that Mr. Podsnap read it all through aloud, laying particular emphasis on the last two lines which are repeated at the end of each verse.

"Amid the burning splendour,
   In all the flashing light,
A whisper warm and tender
   Is softly said to-night;
The fond and fairy hearer,
   Whose beauty is so young,
Thinks never whisper dearer,
   Found music on the tongue,
Thinks never whisper dearer
   Found music on the tongue

One hour past, her being
   Was girlish as her brow;
But all her heart is seeing
   Another picture now!
Her woman's love is shining,
   Her eyes of beauty speak;
See kindled hope reclining
   In blushes on her cheek!
See kindled hope reclining
   In blushes on her cheek!

Fast whirls along the dancing,
   Quick twinkle winning feet:
But faster eyes are glancing,
   And quicker pulses beat!
The girl who went to glisten
   Amid the starry grove,
Had paus'd to look and listen
   And learn'd a woman's love!
Had paus'd to look and listen
   And learn'd a woman's love!"

There were seven other songs quoted, and six of them were on the same scandalous subject of love. In one a Gipsy fortune-teller was saying to all the young Georgianas

"Come hither, maidens! a smile bestow,
   Your future lot I'll quickly show."

In another a maiden "sought the dewy grove" at
an early hour of the morning and, being entirely
unchaperoned, was pursued by a "brave young
hunter boy." It was true that after the hunter boy
had said something about kissing the lady rejoined

"Nor darken with Dishonour's cloud
    The pure bright heav'n of youth"

but still the incident was a thoroughly undesirable
one and never would have occurred if the young
person had stayed where she should have been at
that untimely hour, in bed.

In a third song a young man was deliberately
inviting a young person to elope to foreign parts
and without her parents' consent:

"Night and the moonbeams invite us to flee,
    O'er the glad waters O fly, love, with me!
Then come, love, come to some sunbright isle,
Where peace and pleasures ever smile."

But one construction could be placed on such
language and the only song that was not about
love was, if possible, even more objectionable. It
was called "The Castle and the Cottage," and said
that people were happier in cottages.

"Silken floors adorn that Castle,
    Banner decks its topmost tower;
Sand of snow bestrews the cottage,
    In its lattice many a flower.

Other hearts seek in that Castle
    Pomp with anguish interwove,
Mine the poor and humble cottage
    Richer far in peace and love."

Now Mr. Podsnap had always said that the subject of the poor was "an odious one—not to be
introduced among our wives and young persons"

EWER & CO.'S MUSICAL LIBRARY.

EWER & CO. respectfully request an inspection of their Library, containing about

70,000 DIFFERENT WORKS,

Now available for the use of Subscribers, as it will at once testify the superiority of their Library over any other similar Establishment.

Town Subscribers to EWER & CO.'S Musical Library, Will have an opportunity of becoming acquainted with any of the works which are performed at the Concerts of the different Opera-houses and Musical Societies, or private Concerts in London. All these works are in the Library, not only in the form in which they were originally composed, but also arranged for the Pianoforte, in all degrees of difficulty. No other library possesses such an extensive assortment of these arrangements. Ewer & Co. will give public performances for the introduction of New Music, to which Subscribers will be admitted free.

Country Subscribers to EWER & CO.'S Musical Library, Will have an opportunity of becoming acquainted with such Music as is not generally to be had in the country, especially foreign publications, the newest arrangements of Operas, Sinfonies, Overtures, and Dances, Songs and Part Songs, and the latest compositions of Continental authors; also the works of popular British authors, which are added to the Library immediately on their publication; and Subscribers may thus become acquainted with the whole range of Musical Literature.

EWER & CO. beg particularly to remind Musical Professors and Amateurs, that at their Warehouse they not only find the Newest English Musical Works, but also the

LATEST CONTINENTAL PUBLICATIONS.

EWER & CO., 87, REGENT STREET.

(Sole Proprietor—WILLIAM WITT.)

THE BOOK OF PERFUMES,

BY

EUGENE RIMMEL.

and here they were being shamefully glorified at
the expense of well-to-do people living near Portman
Square, which was much the same as in a castle.

If Georgiana ought to study music at all, which
was doubtful, Mr. Johannes Winkelhaus could provide six pieces, to which there was no objection.
One of them was " 'God Save the Queen,' brilliantly
and gracefully arranged, without being trying to
a moderately advanced performer, and the air is
never lost sight of." Another was " 'Cascade de
Perles,' a very elegant melody set off by passages
which, while full of refinement and beauty, are
completely under the hand and consequently adapted
to the means of players who combine taste with
good execution." Messrs. Ewer & Co. too were
entirely innocuous, as anybody who reads the sample
of their music will discover. As to the disgraceful
Jullien Mr. Podsnap shut up the book with a bang,
and perhaps this was just as well, because under
his very nose in *Our Mutual Friend* was an advertisement of Perfumed Valentines with appropriate
quotations not only from Mrs. Hemans and Shakespeare, who were all very well, but also from Byron
and Moore. Moreover Mr. Rimmel, the serpent
who introduced such things into families, also
boasted of his Rosewater Crackers "a new and
amusing device for evening parties." It would
have been far better if he had confined himself to
his nice, harmless pictures, presumably of Old
London, which could have taught Georgiana
history.

It is a relief to turn from these deplorable and
inflammatory devices to something that could blend
instruction with amusement in the proper propor-
tions. Here in the second number of *Little Dorrit*
(January 1856) is the very thing provided by the
London Stereoscopic Company. "Gentle Reader,
do you possess that charming discovery of Sir David
Brewster's—the Lenticular Stereoscope? If not, at

once add a "New Pleasure" to your home. You
will find it a delightful companion in solitude, and
for social and domestic gatherings, an unfailing
source of intellectual enjoyment. With it no company can ever be *dull*—the themes of conversation
it suggests are as boundless as the pleasure it affords."
And look at the beautiful picture underneath showing the family intellectually enjoying itself with
not one but two instruments. The eldest daughter
has by her side the young man who is paying her
attentions with the full approval of the whiskered
papa. Everybody is taking turns at the instrument, and there is no squabbling. Even the dog
is extending a beseeching paw and wishing that
he might share in the fun. Papa is saying that
they really must get some of the hundred charming views from Switzerland and Pompeii which are
newly advertised. His young daughter on the left,
who is rather a giddy little thing is saying, "Bother
old Pompeii" to herself, and aloud is putting in
a plea for some of the "150 groups of the
most laughable characters" which are also mentioned
in the advertisement. Papa, who can never entirely
resist her, says, "Well, perhaps, but Mamma and I
must have a talk about it. Meanwhile these pictures
of the different courts at the Crystal Palace are
really wonderful."

A few numbers later there is a very special announcement of all the different scenes that can be
bought. First of all come the fifty-five scenes at
the Crystal Palace—all the Courts, a screen of the
Kings and Queens of England, a general view of
the grounds and a correct representation of the
chairman reading an inaugural address to Her
Majesty. Next there are pages and pages of scenery
from various English counties and from France,
Switzerland, Italy, the Rhine and the Pyrenees.
There are theatrical scenes—Miss Heath as Ophelia
and Mr. Harley as Autolycus, and scenes in the

THE LONDON
STEREOSCOPIC COMPANY,

54, CHEAPSIDE (Two Doors West of Bow Church),

AND

313, OXFORD STREET,

(CORNER OF HANOVER SQUARE, TWENTY DOORS WEST OF REGENT SREET.)

Particulars of Subjects, &c., are in the annexed Catalogue.

style of the court of Louis Quatorze which might be a little risky, as they show "the young lovers caught by the duenna." *Our Village* provides a number of "gems," each with "descriptive matter or an appropriate quotation" at the back. There is the Old Church and Squire's house and the fishpond, Old Giles's Grindstone, "Tummas" standing for his picture and "The Old Story" at the village pump. There is a miscellaneous lot called "General Popular Subjects," some of them with titles suggestive of Academy pictures, such as "Happy to take wine with you" evidently a predecessor of Mr. Dendy Sadler. "Miseries of Human Life and Comic Scenes" cost only eighteen pence each, while "Love and Rustic Scenes" are half a crown. The cheaper kind deal mainly with Ireland : Paddy or Pat come into nearly every one of them and there is one called the "Onconvaniences of Single Life." In the others "Impudence" and the "Attempted Kiss" lead up to the "Rustic Wedding." Finally very popular and entertaining at 1*s.* 6*d.* each are subjects of the "Wilkie" character. These are meant for people who are puzzled by those fancy titles that are supposed to be so amusing and like a good plain honest title that tells you exactly what it is all about. Thus "Lady seated at table", "Group of 25 Ladies and Children," "Wooden-legged man at Kenilworth Castle," "Packing Soda Water," and "Girls giving the gardener some Porter." There is some sense in titles like that. If for instance the last scene had been called "Drink to me only with thine eyes" or some such rubbish you never would have known that it was porter; it might have been soda water, and conversely it might have been porter that was being packed. Whatever scenes you chose the *Art Journal* said of them that they were "pure art teaching all classes and orders; gratifying the best informed and delighting the least instructed."

That was, in more modern language, the stuff to give the young person, and if you went to Mr. F. G. Morris, Her Majesty's Publisher, you could make sure of getting it on your walls. Mr. Morris could provide you with "highly important works and prints." For a price "up to eight guineas" there was "Columbus propounding to the Prior of the Franciscan Convent of Rabida his theory of a new world—After Wilkie." "Up to fifteen guineas" he could let you have "the great historical picture, Sir David Baird discovering the body of the Sultan Tippoo Saib after storming Seringapatam" and also after Wilkie. After E. Landseer was "The Retriever, A Favourite Dog, the property of the Accountant-General." You naturally could not hope to get so important a dog for nothing but if you wanted something cheaper two guineas would buy "The Early Dawn. A most sweet and beautiful picture of a genuine 'Mountain Maid' engraved (Con Amóre for it was not a Commission) by S. Cousins from a Drawing by Cristall. A Welsh maiden redolent of health and heart's-ease is going out to her cow milking at 'Early Dawn'."

The Young Person may be assumed to have had the soundest Protestant views and so might have been given a picture which Mr. Ackerman announced with a prodigious flourish of trumpets in *Nicholas Nickleby*.

"TO ALL PROTESTANTS

And by special permission dedicated to Her Most Gracious Majesty the Queen

The Martyrs in Prison"

The martyrs in question were Latimer, Cranmer, Ridley and Bradford, and there was a long poem about them thus described. "The eloquent and soul-stirring verses, the inspiration of the moment upon seeing this *splendid and truly national produc-*

tion, are from *The Times*, and were thence copied into most of the leading Conservative and Protestant journals throughout the country." It may be added that the rascally Radical and Popish journals had the best of the bargain.

Within reasonable limits the young person might be amused by games, and the coming of croquet enlarged the scope of her amusements. The first mention I have found of it is in the first number of *Our Mutual Friend*, May 1864, and the advertiser bears a name still famous, Jaques. There is

Two Prize Medals, 1862.

JAQUES'S CROQUET GAMES.

Prices:—Including the newly-revised Laws of the Game, 8vo. cloth gilt, in Box complete, 15*s.*, 18*s.*, 21*s.*, 25*s.*, 30*s.*, 40*s.*, 50*s.*, 60*s.*, and 5*l.* 5*s.* per set.

Observe.—Each set bears the Manufacturer's Name. Descriptive Price Lists to be had at most Fancy Repositories. Sold Wholesale by the Manufacturers,

JAQUES AND SON,
102, HATTON GARDEN.

a charming picture of a young lady in a crinoline just about to croquet her unfortunate opponent and send his ball flying far away past the mulberry tree, and into the thick laurel bushes. Such at least is clearly her intention, but I am not sure that she will carry it out, for she has not put her pretty foot on the top of her own ball as she ought, and she is holding her hands upside down, the left below the right, in the manner of distinguished batters at baseball. It may be, however, that some

famous player of that early day did hold her mallet
in that way even as rare geniuses hold a golf club.
A croquet set, complete in a box with the newly
revised rules, cost from 15*s.* to £5 5*s.*

The game was new then, but not quite new, for
Mr. Jaques announced that he had won two prize
medals in 1862. *Punch* too, that greatest of British
historians, had already had pictures of it. In
1863 for instance, there is a charming early du
Maurier drawing showing crinolined ladies playing
in a snow storm, hitting with tiny mallets through
enormous hoops hung with bells while at the window, "Pater and Mater expostulate vainly."

In the next year's *Punch*, that of Mr. Jaques's
advertisement, there is a poem on the game—and
a very poor poem too—with what I assume to be an
allusion to du Maurier. It is called, "Croquet—
A parenthesis" and here is the first verse:—

"An English-Frenchman, whom this poem respects,
  Tells me that in my use of circumflex
  Over the "e" in croquêt, as you see,
  I am in no way authorised (*L'Esprit*
  Of the French language asks for, I confess,
  A circumflex when we omit an "s")
  My sole authority's John Ja-ques; so
  I give him up. Ask *him;* he ought to know."

The English-Frenchman who protested to his col-
league must have been du Maurier, but the odd
thing is that in this advertisement in *Our Mutual
Friend* there is no circumflex. The advertisement
appeared in May, the poem in July: so perhaps
John Jaques had learnt better.

As the game became more popular it spread from
out of doors to indoors in a miniature form for
Mr. Jaques is soon announcing Table Croquet and
Carpet Croquet. At the same time he advertises
Squails, Happy Families, Ringoletto and Dartelle
or Drawing Room Archery. Some of these games

THE NICOLL PALETOT,

OR PATENT COAT;

And the original invention, the Registered Paletot (6 and 7 Vic
cap. 6.) The West-end Warerooms for the sale of these graceful
and useful articles of dress are in Regent-street, and extend from
number 114 to number 120 inclusive; and those in the City are at
22, Cornhill, the shipping department being in the rear—viz.,
'Change-alley. Many have assumed the use of the word paletot,
but H. J., and D. NICOLL are the sole Proprietors and Patentees
of either design or material. The prices are one, two, and three
guineas, and according to the climate or purpose for which
they are required.

San Francisco from the south-west, sketched by
Willie & Co., Agents in California for Messrs. Nicoll.

must have been very bad for the furniture, and I do not believe the papa in the stereoscopic picture would have allowed them.

He might have allowed a visit to Mr. Mechi's shop about Christmas time, but only under surveillance, because Mr. Mechi veiled the nature of his wares under a vague grandiloquence. Since "the season is approaching when love and friendship give their tangible testimonials MECHI has taken care to provide abundance of objects for tasteful selection. England has always been renowned for its hearty Christmas liberality, while 'Le jour de l'an' of our lively neighbours the French is equally consecrated to the gifts of affection. Mechi invites a visit from the natives of all countries to his Emporium, which has been pronounced to be the most tastefully arranged and best lighted establishment in London and where they may be sure of putting their kind intentions into an acceptable shape."

The Young Person was, I imagine, usually educated by governesses at home as far as she was educated at all, but sometimes she went to schools such as Miss Twinkleton's at Cloisterham or Miss Tomkins's at Bury, where Mr. Pickwick was imprisoned in a grove of sandwich bags. So when *Edwin Drood* began to appear with its account of Rosa Bud at Miss Twinkleton's School, the Ladies' College at Rochester (which is Cloisterham) calmly identified itself with the Nuns' House and had a half-page advertisement in the second number. "For a hundred years," so it ran, "young ladies have been efficiently educated at the Nuns' House. Within the last three years the London Collegiate system has been introduced, and the instruction now given is on the soundest and most improved system." There were well qualified professors and resident governesses, a gentleman who was an LL.D. with a line all to himself, lectures every week on English Literature and Elementary Physical Science, and the terms were from thirty to fifty guineas a year. I trust that they used at the College Donald Walker's book on Exercises for Ladies. "The work describes and illustrates by numerous drawings the right and wrong positions in Standing, Sitting, Writing, Drawing, Guitar-playing, Harp-playing, Riding, Lying in Bed etc., and the deformities which the wrong positions cause; and it gives all the best exercises to prevent or to correct them, particularly the new and beautiful Indian Sceptre Exercise for the first time published, as well as ample directions as to Walking, Dancing, Gesture and Deportment."

This advertisement was the seizing of a particular and heaven-sent opportunity, and I find no others from girls' schools and only one or two of boys' schools. In the first number of *Dombey* there is a delightful beginning: "Mons. Le Page's French School designed to supersede the necessity of going to France (at the risk of morals) to acquire the Parisian accent." It only refers, however, to a series of books. No schoolmaster emulated the ladies of Rochester by identifying himself with Dr. Blimber, nor for that matter with Mr. Squeers or Mr. Creakle either. Perhaps it is hardly to be wondered at. Neverthe-less there is a touch of the delightful village of Dotheboys, near Greta Bridge, in Mr. Owen's advertisement of his academy at Kennington, which was published in *Nicholas Nickleby*. Mr. Owen's curriculum is nearly as all-embracing as was Mr. Squeers's, and his terms only fifty per cent higher. "Fairlawn House Classical and Commercial Academy, Kennington Lane, Kennington, conducted by Mr. W. Owen. Young gentlemen are boarded and thoroughly grounded in English Literature under the devoted attention of the Principal for thirty guineas per annum, inclusive of books, washing, etc., Mathematical erudition, instruction

in Greek or Latin classics, in the French, Italian, German or other languages or in any accomplishment on the usual terms. The domestic comforts under the discretion and indulgent care of Mrs. Owen."

Were those last words, I wonder, a synonym for brimstone and treacle?

CHAPTER V

THERE is a wonderfully large choice of reading proffered in the Dickens advertisers, magazines and papers and, most of all, books. The advertisements of books seem really remarkable, as presumably giving evidence of the tastes of those who read Dickens. I should hardly, without reflection, have expected so many advertisements of such good books. Perhaps I ought to have expected them because I ought to have remembered that everybody read Dickens. He was a popular author in the widest sense of the word, not merely in the narrower sense in which we are apt to-day rather scornfully to apply it to a "best seller." It is also worth remarking how many of these good books were by writers who were more or less Dickens's contemporaries. There surely can never have been a time when the new books of so many authors were looked forward to with such eager and justifiable anticipation. If Dickens was the most popular of them all he was but *primus inter pares.*

I could fill almost as many pages as there are in this book by setting out advertisements of books which are still famous, and I doubt whether eighty or ninety years hence any one who should be engaged on a similar task could say as much for the present age. There is no cause for alarm, since I am not going to do it, but let me just take a few numbers out of one book, *Dombey and Son.* I have

THE
HISTORY
OF THE
FRENCH
REVOLUTION
BY
M.A.THIERS.

RICHARD BENTLEY, NEW BURLINGTON STREET.

scribbled down on a piece of paper, higgledy-piggledy, the names of the authors who appear, nearly all of them, in the first number of the Dombey Advertiser. I have not sifted them into any sort of classification. Chaucer, Spenser, Shelley, Moore, Byron and then a little drop to Mr. Macaulay's "Lays of Ancient Rome," Leigh Hunt, G. P. R. James, Miss Edgeworth, Fenimore Cooper, Disraeli, Madame D'Arblay, Dumas, Lever, Mrs. Beecher Stow, not only with *Uncle Tom's Cabin* but a "key" to it "containing the documents on which it was founded," Albert Smith, Douglas Jerrold, Martin Tupper, who, as the modern reader may hear with surprise, wrote *The Crock of Gold,* and Dickens himself. There are still three more that I have kept to the last, because something more than the mere names must be given. There is an advertisement of *Mansfield Park* which is described as a "natural, unaffected and beautifully narrated tale", and it is added that Miss Austen has now become a classic. Then there is squeezed into rather a small corner in very small type an announcement of the translation of the works of George Sand by Matilda M. Hays published by E. Churton, of Holles Street. The publisher evidently thinks that he is doing a daring thing that will shock some people and tries in his prospectus to disarm criticism. "In presenting," he says, "a translation of George Sand's works to the English Public, it is the desire of the Translator to afford an opportunity for readers of all classes to judge for themselves, whether the productions of the greatest female genius of the day are deserving that condemnation which it is so much the fashion to attach to them, or whether the time has not come, when an unmerited stigma, having its rise in ignorance, and that dependence upon the judgment of others, which should find no place in an enlightened nation, should be removed, and Madame Dudevant be awarded that position in public opinion, which she has long held with the more intellectual of our fellow countrymen."

In this same number is an advertisement of "*Vanity Fair*, Pen and Pencil Sketches of English Society," the first monthly part being due to appear on New Year's Day, 1847. It is almost as odd to think of a world without *Vanity Fair* as of one without *Pickwick*, and we have something of the same sensation when we look at *David Copperfield* and find the announcement of a "new work," *Shirley*, by Currer Bell. Though Thackeray's name appears as the author it will be seen that it is reinforced by that other name of Michael Angelo Titmarsh which brings back to most of us heavenly memories of *The Rose and the Ring*. The name had been used by him for some time before. In 1840 had been published *The Paris Sketchbook of Mr. Titmarsh*, and in 1841 *Tales and Sketches*, edited and illustrated by Mr. Michael Angelo Titmarsh, which contained the "Yellowplush Papers" from *Fraser's Magazine*.

This announcement is in the fourth number. Eleven months later in the fifteenth number we hear what the critics think of the new story as far as it had gone; The *Dumfries Courier*, with Scottish caution, will not commit itself beyond saying that it was "Decidedly the cleverest periodical of the day." The fact of the reviewer adding that it was "difficult to point out the best passages," arouses the base suspicion that he had not read the book but only looked at the pictures. The *Brighton Herald* is more enthusiastic, saying, "This admirably told tale proceeds as easily as a piece of real life; there is no forcing or jolting or standstill." The young man on the *Morning Chronicle* really lets himself go with a sentence which he contemplated with the utmost complacency. "Everything," he says, "is simple, natural and unaffected. Common sense sits smiling on the top of every page; and the very

NEW WORK BY MICHAEL ANGELO TITMARSH.

On the **First of January, to be continued in Monthly Parts,**

PRICE ONE SHILLING,

WITH NUMEROUS ILLUSTRATIONS ON STEEL AND WOOD,

No. I. OF

Pen and Pencil Sketches of English Society.

———

BY W. M. THACKERAY,

AUTHOR OF "THE IRISH SKETCH BOOK," "JOURNEY FROM CORNHILL TO GRAND CAIRO." OF
"JEAMES'S DIARY" AND THE "SNOB PAPERS" IN "PUNCH"; &c. &c.

———

LONDON:

PUBLISHED AT THE PUNCH OFFICE, 85, FLEET STREET.

J. MENZIES, EDINBURGH; J. M'LEOD, GLASGOW; J. M'GLASHAN, DUBLIN.

AND SOLD BY ALL BOOKSELLERS.

1847.

spirit of society is distilled by the alembic of genius
into drops which sparkle before the reader's eye."

It would be interesting to know who reviewed
for the *Sun*, for he writes as one having authority,
and to say as much as he did after six numbers
marks him as a brave man as well as a good critic.
"If," he says, "Mr. Thackeray were to die to-
morrow, his name would be transmitted down to
posterity by his *Vanity Fair*. Even should the
work never be concluded, the six parts already
published would be sufficient to secure him an im-
mortality. He is the Fielding of the nineteenth
century." I wonder who he was. Perhaps only a
humble little gentleman in Fleet Street who sold
the number as soon as he had reviewed it, and
drank the proceeds. At any rate he made a good
shot and hit the mark.

In the next number the chorus of praise is continued. "We like this Thackeray," the *Western
Times* is good enough to say. "He is a man of
sound mind, with a healthy moral constitution, no
particular affection for romantic rascals and a
mortal hatred of snobs." That however is only
in paltry little two-column type. The *Edinburgh
Review* sprawls right across the page in pompous
splendour. Possibly this review was written by an
eminent person, but it has rather the air of an
extract from Captain Shandon's prospectus for the
Pall Mall Gazette (in *Pendennis*)—the paper, "written
by gentlemen for gentlemen." "The great charm
of this work," says the Edinburgh reviewer, "is
. . . the thoroughbred carelessness with which
the author permits the thoughts and feelings suggested by the situations to flow in their natural
channel, as if conscious that nothing mean or unworthy could fall from him. In a word, the book
is the work of a gentleman." This was evidently
considered the highest possible praise, for the
testimony of the Edinburgh is found quoted again

in several subsequent numbers and even six years later when a new edition is coming out. One page containing this review is reproduced here for the sake of the little drawing by Thackeray of himself. We may compare it with the words of the *Cambridge Chronicle* in a review of Lewis Arundel in the Bleak House Advertiser, "It displays a great deal of that sort of feeling for which we can find no better term than gentlemanly."

Let us now turn to some books that are no longer famous. In *Dombey*, which is a singularly rich mine, there is a full-page announcement of a new monthly work in six parts, "by a lady who has gone through a great deal," to be published by Mr David Bogue, of Fleet Street, at the rate of a shilling a number. Its full title is, *The Greatest Plague of Life, or The Adventures of a Lady in search of a Good Servant by one who has been nearly Worried to Death*. The lady goes on to announce, with a wealth of italics, that she publishes her work, "from motives of benevolence deeming that the troubles she has undergone and the restless nights she has passed, together (she may say) with the distress both of mind and body she has endured, might be interesting as well as instructive to those young wives who are entering upon the thorny path of married life." She adds that she is herself both a wife and the mother of a large family and, that Mr. George Cruickshank has "in the most gentlemanly way" illustrated her book with portraits of the "ungrateful creatures who have successively converted her happy fireside into (if she may be allowed the expression) a *maison de deuil*."

Clearly this book struck a responsive chord in the breasts of the wives and mothers of England to whom it was dedicated, and before the six numbers were completed the lady was hard at work composing another work on a topic of still more universal interest and equally capable of facetious treatment. *Dombey* was still coming out and by no means yet finished when this second work burst on the world, and this time the lady revealed her name with a fine dashing autograph, "Charlotte de Roose." This book was called *Whom to Marry and How to get Married, or the Adventures of a Lady in search of a Good Husband by one who has refused Twenty excellent Offers at least.*

The authoress or her publishers were skilled in the art of playing upon words which was so popular. "The game of matrimony," she says, "is one so difficult for the spinster to play with success that I have long felt that there was a great opportunity for some lady to devote her talents with distinction to the production of a Hymeneal Hoyle, wherein the inexperienced and artless maiden should be taught how to make the most of her hand or—when she is playing high, and a Court Card turns up—how she should on no account refuse the 'Dummy.' This agreeable task has fallen upon me and it will be my object, in the history of my different courtships, to point out to any lady who may be in search of a good husband, how she may—though unable to get one by honours —at least be certain of getting one by tricks."

This book, with Cruickshank pictures, having also proved a success, the lady produced a third called, *The Very Image of his Father, or One Boy more Trouble than a Dozen Girls.*

Clearly, though her style makes the reader feel a little unwell, she supplied a felt want, and has not somebody in our own time sold innumerable copies of a work called *How to be Happy though Married* ?

Facetiousness was the order of the day, and there is a book in the Nickleby Advertiser which I take to have been a fine specimen. At any rate its title was one. It was called *The Handbook of Swindling, by the late Captain Barabbas Whitefeather,* and the author was described as "Late of the Body Guard of His Majesty King Carlos; Treasurer of the British Wine and Vinegar Company; Trustee for the Protection of the River Thames from Incendiaries; Principal Inventor of Poyais Stock; Ranger of St. George's Fields; Original Patentee of the Parachute Conveyance Association; Knight of Every Order of the Fleece. C.U.R. and S.C.A.M.P." The work was edited by John Jackdaw, and illustrated by Phiz.

I should like to have read *Rowland Bradshaw, or The Way to Fame* by the author of *Raby Rattler,* for nothing could be more edifying than his picture on bright green paper. Besides, if the *Sun* thought that Thackeray was the

Publishing every Saturday, price 3d., and in Monthly Parts,

PUNCH,

Or, THE LONDON CHARIVARI.

A

WEEKLY BUDGET

OF

ORIGINAL

WIT AND WHIM,

CRITICAL, POLITICAL,

AND

SATIRICAL.

WITH NUMERQUS

COMIC

WOODCUTS

BY

LEECH, MEADOWS,

CROWQUILL HINE,

AND OTHER

EMINENT ARTISTS.

NOTICES OF THE PRESS.

"The wit and humour of 'Punch' do not evaporate with age. On the contrary, he improves as he grows older. The multitudinous engravings are as full of character, and the writing as pregnant with fun, as ever they were. The same care is observed in the exclusion of whatever is offensive to good morals, or even to good manners. Artist and author never forget that they are working for the amusement of family-circles and parlour firesides. No parent could object its introduction among his children, and while the merry laugh is kindled imperceptibly; the good-humoured satire which calls the smile to the cheek will serve to extirpate many follies and frivolities which have been endured only because they have been sanctioned by society. 'Punch' cannot fail to do excellent service in his generation, and long may he live to make the wise merry, and the merry wise."—Somerset Gazette.

"Piquant and entertaining as usual, without an atom of grossness or immorality."—Maidstone Journal.

"Punch seems to have an inexhaustible vein of humour. At least there is thus far no appearance of falling off. His Letters to his Son, which are among his most novel features, are really exquisite."—Birmingham Adv.

"The most clever and successful publication of its day."—Bristol Mirror.

"Racy, clever, and sarcastic."—Salopian Journal.

"A weekly publication, which, for originality, pungent yet good-natured satire, wit, and readiness, has not been approached of late years by any similar work. We should add, that the pictorial illustrations, with which it is profusely interspersed, partake fully of the same spirit and character as the literary contents."—Bristol Gazette.

"From the first line to the Notices to Correspondents, every page sparkles with wit, and is illumined with the choicest humour. Each folly is caught as it flies, and exposed without one atom of malice; nor is there an expression that could either raise a blush, or excite any other feeling than hilarity and joyousness."—Manchester Adv.

"We at once recommend the reader to go and purchase the work, not only as one of the cleverest, but cheapest, that at present issues from the press."—Sheffield Iris.

"It is impossible to convey any notion, by description, either of the quality or quantity of the wit and humour compressed into this inimitable miscellany. All, therefore, who wish to enjoy a hearty laugh must purchase for themselves."—Liverpool Courier.

"As pungent, witty, and satirical as ever. The work has already attained great success, and deserves it. The woodcut illustrations are of first-rate excellence, and redolent of fun and humour."—Leeds Times.

*** The Third Volume, containing more than 1000 Illustrations, is now ready; and Vols. 1 and 2 are always kept on Sale.

Now publishing,   price Threepence,

Punch's Almanack for 1843!

BRIMFUL OF FUN AND JOKES!!
AND EMBELLISHED WITH NEARLY ONE HUNDRED HUMOROUS CUTS!!!

Now Ready, price 3s. 6d. bound in roan,

PUNCH's POCKET-BOOK for 1843.
Also, price 5s. bound in cloth,

PUNCH's LETTERS TO HIS SON.
EDITED BY DOUGLAS JERROLD. WITH ILLUSTRATIONS BY MEADOWS.

OFFICE, 13, WELLINGTON STREET, STRAND.

Fielding of the nineteenth century, the *Weekly Times* reviewer went one better, and said that Rowland Bradshaw reminded him favourably of Fielding. Yet I shall have to go I fear to the British Museum to read those "humorous sketches of the *élite* of the neighbourhood of Manchester." Incidentally compliments on this magnificent scale were not so uncommon as might be supposed, for of an unknown author, who wrote a book called *Matrimonial Jumbles* in the 'fifties, it is said, "In power of description the author equals Dickens."

Tom Racquet and his Three Maiden Aunts sounds, as they say, "intriguing", and another book having a pleasant title is *Raphael's Royal Book of Fate, or Queen Elizabeth's Oracle of Future Events*—with a large folding coloured plate containing "sixty-four mystical emblems, relating to riches, love, marriage, dreams foretold, and all subjects of Fate, Chance and Mortal Destiny; with 4,000 answers to most important questions in Human Life." It sounds exciting, but I am afraid it only corresponds to the automatic machines, bearing the picture of a gipsy, from which for one penny the love-sick housemaid can still discover whether she will marry a dark gentleman or a fair one.

Not only were new books freely advertised but also new newspapers. In 1843 we find *Mr. Punch*, still very nearly new, with a picture of himself which strikes us to-day as more or less uncharacteristic. In January 1847 the *Daily News*, of which Dickens had for a short time been editor in the previous year, takes a page to itself to announce the remarkable fact that it can be bought for three pence. There are more daily papers published in the City of New York than in all England, Scotland and Ireland put together, and what is the cause? Price! Till the *Daily News* was founded, a daily London paper was "a costly luxury, in which only the wealthy could indulge," but now the *Daily News*

H

is bigger than some of its expensive contemporaries
and "looks for support, not to a comparatively few
readers at a high price, but to many at a low
price."

It did not have the field to itself, for a few months
later the advent of a new daily paper is announced.
On the first of February 1848 the first number of
the *London Telegraph* is to appear and it will cost
three pence and be published at noon every day.
It will have expresses by the electric telegraph from
important towns as much as two hundred miles
away, thus, " in reality abolishing time and space,"
and " contributions from the most learned men of
the day."

This is a brief, businesslike announcement,
crowded economically into half the space taken by
the *Daily News*.   If we want something more florid
we must go to the advertisement of *The Lady's
Newspaper*, a new illustrated weekly to appear for
the first time on Saturday, January 2, 1847, price
sixpence.   Here is the manner of Captain Shandon
to the life, save that the Captain always brought
in the battle of Waterloo and " had never known the
Duke to fail."   I cannot, alas! rise to the beautiful
red letters, but I can reproduce the spacings and
the varied type with which the writer decorates the
two pages of his prospectus.   And if it is not a chaste
and classical composition, I should like to know
what is.

Other papers, new or in a new form, that we find
advertised are *The Field* in *Bleak House* (1857)
and *The Athenæum*, in an enlarged form, in *Edwin
Drood* (1870).   *The Field* boasts of illustrations by
Leech and Hablot Browne, who was Phiz, and
devotes itself to "Agriculture and health-giving
pursuits generally."   *The Athenæum's* table of contents looks, I must say, formidably stodgy, amply
justifying John Finsbury's famous criticism "The
Athæneum, Golly, what a paper!"

Published every SATURDAY. commencing Saturday, Jan. 2, 1847:

THE LADY'S NEWSPAPER,

BEAUTIFULLY ILLUSTRATED,

WITH DESIGNS BY THE FIRST ARTISTS, ENGRAVED BY E. LANDELLS.

(Twenty-four Folio Pages, Seventy-two Columns, printed in New Type on Fine Paper),

STAMPED, PRICE SIXPENCE.

DOES it not appear extraordinary that our literature of every kind should possess so meagre a claim on the attention of

THE LADIES,

considered with reference to their peculiar tastes, feelings, and pursuits? Out of above six hundred Newspapers, not one is specially intended or adapted for their use! This is a great, a startling, and, we must add, anything but a creditable fact; the more obviously so, since a lovely, amiable, and highly intellectual

QUEEN

is at the head of the Nation; and WE therefore now make our bow, and come forward as the projectors of

THE LADY'S NEWSPAPER,

to supply the deficiency.

To the

MAIDENS OF ENGLAND

We say,

BUY THE LADY'S NEWSPAPER!

Are not our British Maidens both the Admiration and the Hope of the present generation; buds of loveliness, that by

" ———— Summer's ripening breath,"

are to continue to our land the blessings of the past? All their most cherished Studies, Amusements, Accomplishments, and Pursuits; Literature, Music, Drawing and Painting, Floriculture, Popular Science, Fancy Needlework, Fashions and the Philosophy of Adornment, the Dance, Archery, all the Week's News, &c. will be found in this Journal.

WIVES OF ENGLAND,

BUY THE LADY'S NEWSPAPER!

In its columns will be found all that is most interesting and serviceable to a well-regulated *Menage*. Need we say more?

MOTHERS,

We appeal to you in profound sincerity, when we urge you to

BUY THE LADY'S NEWSPAPER!

The intellectual advancement of a family is, of course, of paramount consideration: and we can offer the contributions of all the most gifted female spirits of the age, together with a long list of writers of the other sex, who have done honour to our literature. The Nursery and the management of a Family, will, of course, form an especial department.

LADIES MOVING IN FASHIONABLE LIFE,

BUY THE LADY'S NEWSPAPER!

We appeal to you, as the fairest ornaments of our Court and Country, on all the topics (and how numerous they are!) which most interest you.

And now we turn to those most concerned in the welfare of the amiable sex, and say to

HUSBANDS, LOVERS, FATHERS, SONS, & BROTHERS,

BUY THE LADY'S NEWSPAPER!

For do you imagine that you could make them a more acceptable offering? And briefly, to both Sexes, if *resident in the country*, it would be impossible to conceive a more instructive or delightful way of passing the time, than by a perusal of this attractive publication.

As the

FASHIONS

will be given WEEKLY, direct from PARIS, ALL those who are immediately and Professionally interested, namely, Milliners and Dressmakers, will of course

BUY THE LADY'S NEWSPAPER!

In conclusion, it will be the aim of the Conductors, not only to exclude all that is objectionable, but to be lavish of information on the useful and elegant; and in an earnest and unswerving spirit to advocate those high truths, Religious and Moral, of which WOMAN, unfettered by ambition, and comparatively free from the turmoils of the World, has ever been the faithful Guardian.

THE LADY'S NEWSPAPER will be Published at the Office, No. 294, Strand, each SATURDAY; and may be had of all Booksellers and Newsvenders in Town and Country.

PRICE SIXPENCE.

OFFICE, 294, STRAND.

It had "dramatic gossip," but not, we may suspect, of the kind that John, the admirer of the Great Vance, would have appreciated.

Another most respectable magazine, *The Fortnightly*, edited by George Henry Lewis, announces its arrival in *Our Mutual Friend* (1865) and declares itself free of all party trammels; its only consistency will be "in aiding progress in all directions." Even more blameless and self-satisfied is the Editor of the *Illustrated London News*, who remarks that he "has not pandered to the prejudices of the high nor the passions of the lower orders of Society, but taking the higher ground of neutrality has contented himself with the advocacy of justice morality and truth." He has done it in poetry, as well as in prose, as may be seen on the preceding page. Everybody is so dreadfully respectable that one begins to understand why poor ignorant foreigners called us a race of hypocrites. For making the best of both worlds there is nothing to equal the advertisement of *Bell's Weekly Messenger*. "Without undue reflection on their competitors the Proprietors of *Bell's Messenger* may be allowed to observe that many journals have obtained large circulations from the mere fact of their containing masses of news, without reference to the dangerous and irreligious tendencies of the principles studiously inculcated in their columns. *Bell's Weekly Messenger* has for years ceased to be published on Sunday. It infringes on no portion of the Sabbath; nor, with the consent of the Proprietors, are any copies sold on the Sunday. At the same time, being made up from the latest sources of intelligence up to Saturday evening, it contains to the full as much information as the Sunday newspapers, which, though they bear, with an unnecessary contempt of the sanctity of the day, the imprint of Sunday, are nevertheless all of them made up in the same manner on Saturday." If Mr. Pecksniff, Mr. Chadband and Mr. Stiggins had been the directors of a newspaper they could hardly have done better than that.

Captain Shandon's prospectus of the *Pall Mall Gazette* in *Pendennis* has been mentioned before in this chapter. It is rather amusing to come across the prospectus of the real *Pall Mall Gazette*, which appeared in *Our Mutual Friend* in February of 1865, fifteen years after *Pendennis*. It is not by any means so bold or dashing a composition as Captain Shandon's. It does not say that it is addressed to the "Gentlemen of England," but, more cautiously to "educated men and women." It lays stress on the fact that it will avoid excess of words and its reports will be "written in plain English," since "the lessons to be found in many an accident of human life or social polity are lost in the turgid language in which they are commonly narrated." No budding newspaper could, however, compete in splendour or profuseness of advertisement with *Lloyd's Weekly* in the time of Douglas Jerrold's editorship, which was the time of *Bleak House*. In 1846 there had appeared, duly advertised in *Dombey*, *Jerrold's Weekly Newspaper*, of which he was part proprietor and editor, but it had not been a success and changed first its name and then its owner. In 1852 he became editor of *Lloyd's Weekly*, and so remained till he died in 1857. There is nothing very particular about the writing of the advertisements but the pictures, three of them in one number, are beautiful. In one we have a scene at an inn. Two customers are sitting at a small table. One of them is wholly obscured except as to his legs by *Lloyd's Weekly Newspaper*, which is unfolded to its uttermost limits, and he is reading it with frenzied interest. The other, who is waiting for it, has put on his tall hat as a hint that he has little time to spare, and is looking angrily at his unconscious neighbour. One hand is clutching at his umbrella in a furious

WAITING FOR LLOYD'S NEWSPAPER.

THE RED-HOT POLITICIAN

THE LATEST INTELLIGENCE

EXHIBITION

OF

INDUSTRY OF ALL NATIONS;

TO BE HELD IN LONDON IN 1851.

HER MAJESTY'S COMMISSIONERS for the Promotion of the EXHIBITION OF THE WORKS OF INDUSTRY OF ALL NATIONS, to be holden in 1851, having had the various subjects of their inquiry under their anxious consideration, are now prepared to state, for the information of the public, the progress they have made in determining on the different points referred to in their announcement of the 11th January last.

The decisions they have been able to come to have been necessarily limited by their present want of knowledge as to what pecuniary means will be placed at their disposal; and the shortness of the time, during which this vast organization will have to be completed renders it imperative upon the Commissioners to make an earnest appeal to the country, to enable them as soon as possible, to know upon what amount of subscriptions they may ultimately rely.

The scale upon which this important undertaking will be conducted, must depend entirely on the amount of pecuniary support which it shall receive from the public. Her Majesty's Commissioners appeal with confidence to all classes of the community, to enable them to make such liberal arrangements as will ensure the success of this undertaking, in a manner worthy of the character and position of this country, and of the invitation which has been given to the other nations of the world to compete with us in a spirit of generous and friendly emulation.

The Commissioners have fixed upon the 1st day of May, 1851, for opening the Exhibition

The Commissioners will be prepared to receive and take care of, at the expense of the Commissioners, all articles which may be sent to them, and delivered at a place to be named by the Commissioners in London, on or after the 1st of January, 1851, and will continue so to receive goods until the 1st of March inclusive; after which day no further goods will be received.

Her Majesty has been graciously pleased to grant a site for this purpose on the south side of Hyde Park, lying between the Kensington Drive and the Ride commonly called Rotten Row.

From the approximate estimate which the Commissioners have been able to make, they believe that the Building ought to cover a space of from 16 to 20 Acres, or about One million of Square Feet.

The Productions of all Nations will be exhibited together, under one General Classification.

The Articles exhibited will be divided into Four Sections, as before announced, and a Classified List, together with general instructions affecting each Department, are appended. Her Majesty's Commissioners wish to express their grateful sense of the valuable assistance which they have received in drawing up that List from the Members of the Sectional Committees.

The Building will be provided to the Exhibitors free from rent, and will be fire-proof.

Exhibitors will be required to deliver their objects at their own charge and risk, at the Building in the Park; but no charges of any kind will be made whilst they remain there.

Colonial and Foreign productions will be admitted without paying duty, for the purposes of exhibition, but not for internal consumption. Her Majesty's Commissioners of Customs will consider all such Articles as Bonded Goods; and Her Majesty's Commissioners for the Exhibition of 1851 will make suitable arrangements for their reception.

Her Majesty's Commissioners are desirous that there should be complete local organization, and that the Local Committees, wherever formed, should themselves collect the Subscriptions within their own districts. The Local Committees should advertise all Subscriptions they receive, and defray all local expenses, paying such commission for collection as they may think necessary.

Her Majesty's Commissioners think that the same complete system of organization should be extended as much as possible to the British Colonies.

Subscriptions should be paid to the Treasurers of Local Committees, and by them transferred to the General Fund at the Bank of England, in the names of A. K. Barclay, Esq., W. Cotton, Esq., Sir J. W. Lubbock, Bart., S. M. Peto, Esq., M.P., and Baron Lionel de Rothschild, M.P.

Her Majesty's Commissioners having undertaken the absolute control over the expenditure of all money that may come into the hands of their Treasurers, have made arrangements for auditing accounts, and ensuring the strictest economy.

I

CONTENTS.

grip: the other is drumming on the table. On the wall of the room is a notice particularly requesting gentlemen not to detain the paper.

In another picture a gentleman is reading *Lloyd's* while having his hair cut. The hairdresser cannot resist the temptation to look over his shoulder with the result that he runs the scissors into his victim's head. It is called, "The Red-Hot Politician." The third and pleasantest of all, called "The Latest Intelligence", shows two young ladies out for a drive in the park. In the background is the crystal dome of the Great Exhibition, but they have no eyes for it, since they are engrossed in *Lloyd's*. So is their negro footman in the dickey behind who is reading eagerly over their shoulders. The date is too late; otherwise I should like to think that the picture represented Amelia and Becky Sharp going out for a drive in Mr. Sedley's carriage, under the escort of Black Sambo. And apropos here is a full-page advertisement issued by the Commissioner of the Great Exhibition to their public and their potential subscribers.

The Christmas number of *London Society* is interesting as introducing names that sound old now but doubtless sounded new then, H. J. Byron, E. J. Poynter and G. du Maurier who illustrated "Christmas in the Streets with *Mr. Punch.*"

Finally, though it should not perhaps strictly belong to this chapter, let us look, in the Bleak House Advertiser, at the rapturous puff by Mrs. S. C. Hall of the engraving of the great Mr. Frith's picture called "The Village Pastor." Mrs. Hall was a busy writer of novels, and her husband was also in the literary line and wrote a book called *The Baronial Halls, Picturesque Edifices and Ancient Churches of England*. The picture is founded on Goldsmith's poem, from which there are several quotations, but Mrs. Hall becomes even more poetical in her prose about Mr. Frith. He is "entirely a painter of English life; which, though he never so much refines upon as to depart from its essential character and qualities, in his hands is purified from every taint of coarseness and vulgarity. He has a great deal of sentiment, which fortunately is based upon the soundest principles of art," and so on. She makes a passing allusion to those who insinuate that the village parson's position is not what it was; "those who send forth these tales and seek to pollute the fresh and pure waters of life by evil principles and doubtful imaginings, know nothing of the actual state of our rural districts; but write of what they desire rather than what they know." At any rate in those villages, "where the railroad whistle is as distant as the eagle's scream" the vicar is still everything to the poor man.

There follow four pages, in which all the principal figures in the picture are described. She takes the various groups and goes through them as if she were Mrs. Jarley with her waxworks. First there is the pastor himself and the child plucking his gown, and the mother of the child and the husband of the mother, whose "attitude and bearing is in admirable keeping with the scene." There is another young mother, with her infant in her arms, "endeavouring to direct its attention to the pastor," and another "stunted" child with its grandmother who appears to be saying that she has listened to the pastor for a great many Sabbaths.

Next there is the background—the young Squire and his wife and an old man who has a petition to make. The wife tries to melt her husband but "that haughty brow and firm-set mouth will not relax!" Near the churchyard gate is a "group of old calculating men." Mrs. Hall is not quite sure as to what Mr. Frith meant them to be calculating, but she has various solutions to offer. Some of them are of rather a painful character, since there is in the group an old gentleman in spectacles, "the

very personification of doubt," and, it *may* be that
even amongst the gravestones "secular feelings
have for a time rendered them forgetful."

Behind these arguers is a pair of lovers, the man
"comely and handsome and earnest," the maiden
"modest and devout." Their conduct is so admirable that it is not out of place in a churchyard and
"never," Mrs. Hall feels assured, "was a gentle
love passage more sweetly rendered." Behind these
again is another couple, a widow and a daughter,
rapidly fading away. "It is impossible by description to do justice to the sentiment of these two
figures," but unfortunately Mrs. Hall tries to do so
to the extent of a page or more. Enough to say
that Mr. Frith "exhibits the Artist as a great and
triumphant moral teacher."

CHAPTER VI

SMOKING

AN American gentleman who has lately written a learned book on Dickens remarks that "the weed is not nearly so ubiquitous in his work as the bottle." That is no doubt true of Dickens, and it is equally true of the time at which he wrote. Smoking was an occupation for the harness-room or the kitchen rather than the dining-room. Apart from that we feel that Dickens, though he was a smoker, had not the same zest in thinking of cigars as of milk punch. He was as moderate in one respect as in the other, but there was for him in imagination no ecstatic glamour of friendliness and cheerfulness round smoking as there was round drinking. He had not in him any of that intense feeling that inspired Calverley to write "Here's to thee, Bacon." If he had there certainly would have been smoking on the festal days at Manor Farm: or Tom Smart would have lighted his pipe when safe indoors from the wind in that delicious little inn on the edge of Marlborough Downs: So would Short and Codlin as they came out of the rain into "The Jolly Sandboys" before the heavenly stew was ready. Think, in short, of anyone of those many scenes of inimitable warmth and snugness and jollity of which the books are full and see in how few of them tobacco plays any part. Dickens seems to have thought of smoking as something soothing and contemplative but having no direct connection with conviviality.

THE NICOLL PALETOT,

Or, PATENT COAT, and the Original Invention, the REGISTERED PALETOT (6 & 7 Vic. c. 65).

The Warerooms for the sale of these graceful and useful Articles of Dress are in Regent-street, Nos. 114 to 120 inclusive, and at 22, Cornhill, City, the shipping department being in the rear—viz., 'Change Alley.

CAPE OF GOOD HOPE, where Messrs. N coll have an Agency.

BRADBURY AND EVANS, PRINTERS, WHITEFRIARS.

Sometimes he thought of it as positively unpleasant or, as our American gentleman puts it, "He
was not insensitive to the filthiness of smoking."
Certainly he was not insensitive to the habits of
some of the American gentlemen of his own day
connected with tobacco, as witness Martin Chuzzlewit
passim. There was something rather low and vulgar
about smoking. When we first meet Mr. Bob Sawyer
we are told that he had "that sort of slovenly smart-
ness and swaggering gait, which is peculiar to young
gentlemen who smoke in the streets by day, shout
and scream by night, call waiters by their Christian
names, and do various other acts and deeds of an
equally facetious description." Mr. Benjamin Allen
too had "rather a mildewy appearance and emitted
a fragrant odour of full-flavoured Cubas."

Some Dickensian statisticians, of amazing
though possibly misguided industry, could no doubt
enumerate all the characters that smoked, and
probably the sum total of them is considerable;
but the fact remains, I think, that tobacco plays
an insignificant part in the books and that we think
of very few of the characters with pipes or cigars
in their mouths. Eugene Wrayburn smoked a
good many cigars, but he did so chiefly to emphasize
the cool insolence of his gentility; he smoked with
a tantalizing deliberation while poor, tiresome
plebeian Bradley Headstone raved at him. David
Copperfield only smoked once after that fatal dinner
that he gave to Steerforth and his two friends, and
we know what came of his experiment. We cannot
imagine Mr. Pickwick smoking, though we know
that with his customary amiability he told the
gentleman in the mosaic studs at the "Magpie and
Stump" that he liked it very much, though he was
no smoker himself. Even so when the gentleman
said that smoke was board and lodging to him, Mr.
Pickwick could not help thinking that "if it were
washing too it would be all the better." Mr. Weller,

senior, was of course a pipe smoker; we know from his son, as a proof of his philosophy, that when Mrs. Weller broke his pipe, he stepped out and got another. Yet in that very remark we see that he was not a really hardened smoker, or he would surely not have had to go out to get another. He did not carry a pipe about with him, and we have further evidence of that fact in the Fleet scene, when Mr. Weller remarked to Sam, "I think a pipe would benefit me a good deal, could I be accommodated, Sammy?" No doubt he smoked a long church-warden, difficult to carry about, but still there is certain lack of thoroughness.

The villainous Rigaud in *Little Dorrit* smoked cigarettes, but then he was a melodramatic villain with whom a cigarette has always been part of the regular stock in trade. Mr. Montague Tigg, who was also a villain though an amusing one, smelt of stale tobacco when poor, and no doubt smoked large cigars when he was rich. John Jasper, the most tremendous villain of all, smoked opium, and a number of more or less virtuous people smoked pipes now and then. I will not prolong the list, but generally speaking the smoke was not part of the man as the cheroot was of Colonel Newcome, the pipe of Warrington or the regalia of Rawdon Crawley. Dickens had not the same kindliness towards tobacco that Thackeray had, and this seems a pity, because no one in the world could have made it so heavenly as he could, had he had the mind to it.

If there is not much tobacco in the books there is less in the advertisements. This rarity is illuminating, and seems to show that we smoke a great deal more than did our ancestors. That kind of reasoning can no doubt be pushed too far. There is, as has been said, hardly anything about soap in the advertisements, and it would be rash to assume that our ancestors did not wash. Still it was apparently not worth while to appeal to the great heart of the people about tobacco, for such advertisements as my imperfect researches have discovered appeal to the more or less rich. There are just two or three cigar merchants, and there is Mr. Inderwick with his meerschaum pipes, and that is positively all I can find. The cigar merchants advertise little, and Mr. Inderwick, though a regular advertiser, takes up as a rule a very humble amount of space. Oddly enough, considering that the habit of smoking must have spread steadily as time went on, the tobacco advertisements are decidedly more frequent in *Martin Chuzzlewit* than in the later books, and the one piece of literature on smoking is advertised in *Nickleby*. This is a work illustrated by Phiz and called "A Paper —— of Tobacco. Treating of the Rise, Progress, Pleasure and Advantages of Smoking, with remarks on the use and abuse of the Fascinating Weed, Anecdotes of Distinguished Smokers, Items on Pipes and Tobacco Boxes. And an Essay, Tritical, Critical, Practical and Theoretical on Snuff by Joseph Fume."

It is in *Chuzzlewit* that Mr. Inderwick (of Princes Street, Leicester Square and Constantinople), having advertised more modestly in *Nickleby*, launches out into a long treatise on meerschaum, which he says is "a species of mineral earth called by the Tartars *keef kil*, found only in its pure state near Caffa in the Peninsula of the Heracleatæ." He goes on to give a description of his expedition to the promontory, "a wild and fearful scene such as Shakespeare has described in his *Lear*."

"Some time," he says, "after the capture of the Crimea by the Russians, J. I. and Co. were induced to visit the capital of the Crimea, which they found in a state of desolation. The melancholy devastations committed by the Russians would draw tears down the cheeks of the Tartars and extort many a sigh from the Anatolian Turks, who resort to Caffa for commercial purposes, and cannot fail to excite the indignation of every enlightened people. Finding no hope of making any arrangement during Paul's reign, J. I. determined on sending his partner, who is a native of Balaclava in Tartary, together with a tribe consisting of Calmuks, Tartars, and Greeks, on a Syrian route, in search of this scarce mineral." We are then told at some length how the expedition went by Jerusalem and the Dead Sea, where they found one pit, but to their great disappointment it contained magnesia, which was apparently fatal. However, "having at length by the interference of Royalty gained permission to explore the pits of the Crimea", Mr. Inderwick will now have ever afterwards a regular and superior supply, and the pipes cost from two to five guineas each.

After occupying quite a large space with this account of his adventures Mr. Inderwick drew in his horns and just mentioned his meerschaum pipes in the smallest possible amount of room in various of the succeeding advertisers. Once he broke out on the subject of the Cigar Divan, a romantic term which reminds us now of Prince Florizel of Bohemia but reminded Mr. Inderwick of the Duke of Orleans. "Smoking Divans A La Orleans, Fitted up from 5 to 1,000 guineas each: It having become the fashion since the late lamented death of the Duke of Orleans for Noblemen and Gentlemen to have fitted up *Smoking Divans* for the enjoyment of their friends, as well as Libraries for their instruction, J. INDERWICK and Co. beg to acquaint Noblemen and Gentlemen that they will undertake to fit up their *Sanctum* or *Salon*, in the Style of Oriental Luxury, with Robes of the Asiatic Order, together with Howdahs from Lucknow and Bengal; Egyptian, Arabian and Turkish Tchibouques, Meerschaums from the Crimea, Kalyhams from Persia, enriched with precious stones and rings of Damask work! Mouthpieces of the *rarest Amber*, with gold-enamelled centres." Even with this modest display Mr. Inderwick was for months and years at a time the only advertiser of tobacco in the Dickens books. Indeed, I can only find a cigar merchant or two to keep him company.

One is Mr. Edwin Wood, of 69, King William Street, who described his stock of cigars in *Martin Chuzzlewit*. The prices are instructive and make one think, as do so many other things in these advertisers, that one has come into the world too late. How delightfully easy it would have been to cut a dash when "Genuine Havanas" cost only 18*s.* and "superior ones" 22*s.* The price is presumably "per hundred", though this is not actually stated. "Regalias" cost no more than the "genuine", but there were some, by far the most gorgeous of all, that cost 35*s.* On the other hand there were some much cheaper. These were the "Far famed Old Cubas" at 12*s.* In the same number is advertised Howse's Pink Champagne at 27*s.* a dozen, and a little later Betts's "Patent" Brandy at a price unknown. These three would have gone well together to make a roystering evening, though possibly an uncomfortable morning. And here perhaps I may interpolate, as of kindred interest, some prices of wine at a rather later time, that of *Our Mutual Friend*. They are from an advertisement of the famous Sandeman's. His Port from the wood was 12*s.* a gallon. Champagne was from 36*s.* to 60*s.* a dozen, Cliquot and Ruinart 80*s.* Hock and Moselle 30*s.* to 84*s.* Sherry 12*s.* a gallon.

In *David Copperfield*, Louis Silberberg announces that he has opened premises in Fleet Street "with a stock of the Finest Havana Cigars selected with great judgement and care; also with a fresh importation of his justly celebrated Bremen cigars at 14*s.* per pound, the quality of which has given universal satisfaction for the last four years." He has also an entirely new tobacco imported to him direct, called Tabac de Nepaul, the flavour of which he can safely rely upon in giving great satisfaction to the public.

I wish I could have found something about those "Penny Pickwicks" which enjoyed an equivocal fame for years after the immortal work was published, but I cannot. No doubt they themselves provided their own most poignant advertisement.

CHAPTER VII

FOR THE HEAD

I MUST needs divide the Dickens advertisers in a rather arbitrary way. Mr. Moses said that his trousers "would honour the legs." Here is a chapter devoted to people who propose in one way or another to honour the head.

At the top of the list must come "The Gentleman's real head of hair or invisible peruke." I put it first not because of its intrinsic beauty, though that, as the picture shows, is considerable, but because of its faithfulness and unchanging character. Other advertisers are comparatively capricious: they change both their words and their pictures. Not so the sole inventor of the peruke, Mr. F. Browne, of 47 Fenchurch Street. He has always the same modest little quarter of a page, the same picture, the same space for measurements to be made according to his "infallible method." His words, always the same, are few and well chosen. "The principle upon which this Peruke is made is so superior to everything yet produced that the Manufacturer invites the honour of a visit from the Sceptic and the Connoisseur, that one may be convinced and the other gratified by inspecting this and other specimens of the Perruqueian Art." They recur again and again, in book after book, like a gentle haunting refrain. Pillmakers may rise and fall, Moses may sing his swan song, but the Gentleman's invisible peruke goes on for ever. "The charge for this unique head of hair is only £1 10s."

A neighbour of the peruke in several advertisers is the Atrapilatory or Liquid Hair Dye, "the only dye that really answers for all colours and does not require re-doing but as the hair grows, as it never fades or acquires that unnatural red or purple tint

common to all other dyes." The same maker provides for hair that is falling off the tremendous-sounding dual remedy of Botanic Water and Bear's Grease, and he is also the maker of the tooth-pick brush and the Double anti-pressure nail brush.

The man who makes these things we assume for a long time to be an entirely respectable and virtuous person, an "honest tradesman," like Jerry Cruncher. In reality he is a snake in the grass. Suddenly, without a word of warning, in the second number of *David Copperfield*, he makes an unprovoked assault upon the "Gentleman's real head of hair

or invisible peruke." He issues his audacious challenge with an "Invisible Ventilating head of hair." It is almost of the same price—"from $1\frac{1}{2}$ guineas"; and has almost the same device for self measurement. These knavish tricks might have been endured, but it has almost the same picture, and that is an outrage. I am convinced that its ruffianly creator went, attired in a black mask, to see the

artist who had drawn the original peruke and
seduced him from his allegiance. There is an
unmistakable touch about both pictures but the
new one gives a halo to the funny little gentleman
depicted.

There is not only a gentleman, there is also a
thin sad lady portrayed, with a monstrous lack of
chivalry, as bald as an egg. The villain might have
shouted his Botanic Water and his Bear's Grease
as loudly as he liked and we would have wished him
well, but this is too much, and now we hope that he
will be ruined. But will he? We tremble for our
old friend Mr. F. Browne and wonder how he will
face the danger and what kind of counter-attack he
will make. We ought to have known him better.
He makes no counter-attack; he does not show by
as much as the wink of an eyelid that he is conscious
of the intruder; his picture, his words, everything
remain the same.

In several numbers the two advertisements appear
simultaneously, facing one another from opposite
pages, like two armies drawn up for battle with a
valley in between them. Then in one number they
are on the same page, but it is the gentleman's
real head of hair that is above and the invisible
head that is below. That settles the issue;. the
ventilating head becomes invisible; it disappears
altogether, and Mr. F. Browne is left in possession
of the field, as wholly unchanged in the hour of
triumph as he was in that of battle.

The most eloquent friend of the head is Mr. Rowland with his Macassar Oil and his Kalydor. Apart
from the benefits which he conferred on the human
race by making their hair, their complexion and their
teeth so shining and beautiful, Mr. Rowland has
this claim to favour that he was apparently one of
the first to see the advantages of a Dickensian
Christmas. The other advertisers were stupid and
stick-in-the-muddish. Here was Dickens writing

his *Chimes* and his *Christmas Carols* and, far the best of all, his Christmas party at Dingley Dell, and only Mr. Rowland took fire from him. It is true that Dickens said a great deal about good cheer and very little indeed about presents. In all the Dingley Dell chapters I can think of no presents save two. There was the gold watch and chain that Mr. Pickwick gave to Mrs. Trundle, and that was a wedding present. There were the five shillings and the two old coats that Mr. Winkle offered to give Sam, and that was only in the agony of the moment when the ice was so slippery that he needed support. Still, any go-ahead tradesman would surely have seen that a man in a hearty Christmas-like frame of mind was just the one to unbutton his breeches pockets. Certainly Mr. Mechi did allude to presents, and one gentleman advertised, "Christmas. Rich and full flavoured Port Wine, 32*s*. a dozen." Otherwise advertisers merely repeated their old stories, and not even Mr. Morison thought of saying that there was nothing like a pill after a Christmas dinner.

Mr. Rowland on the other hand, though now and then in summer he declared his preparations to be useful on the "aquatic excursion", seems to have saved up for the December number and always came out strong on these occasions. His style improved as it went along. He begins with a puny head-line, "Acceptable presents" followed in tiniest print by the statement, "The present season is hallowed by one of the most delightful offices of Friendship and Affection, the interchange of Gifts." He then delicately points out that a purely useful present gives no evidence of taste nor a purely useless one of judgment on the giver's part, but that these requisites are combined in that glorious trinity— Macassar, Kalydor and Odonto. A few years later he is altogether freer in technique and more sure of himself. He has a bold heading, "Christmas" and then proceeds, "The Yule Log (specially printed in old English characters) will soon burn ruddily on the hearth; the tables be spread with luxurious cheer; many guests will assemble; the toast go round; the song enchant all hearers; the cheek of beauty will glow; the heart of youth will palpitate with love and joy; and finally

> A measure—a measure
> For fair dames and gentlemen!

will resound through the glorious halls.

It is at this period of festivity and mirth that the fair and youthful are more than usually desirous of shining in

PERSONAL ATTRACTION

under the gaze of many friends and the following unrivalled discoveries for the toilet are necessarily called into increased requisition.

The Patronage of Royalty and the Aristocracy throughout Europe and their well known infallible efficacy render them a peculiarly

ELEGANT AND SEASONABLE PRESENT."

That is a fine passage and appears the more flamboyant because underneath it is our dear old friend the Invisible Peruke, unmoved by the season, unmoved by anything, quiet, dignified, persistent, flowing along like a big silent river.

Skip on another four years to another Christmas, and Mr. Rowland is at it again. "The exuberance of the feelings amid scenes of gaiety induces the fair and youthful to shine to advantage under the gaze of many friends, and therefore to devote increased attention to the duties of the toilet. Macassar Oil imparts a transcendant lustre and Kalydor a radiant bloom, while Odonto bestows a pearl-like whiteness." "All wery capital," Mr.

Rowland, but you need not think you have crushed and shaken off the Gentleman and his Invisible Peruke. There he is again next door to you. I wonder what you thought of him. Did you despise him as a dull unimaginative dog or did he make you feel uneasy? "He don't say nothing, he must know something." Had he got the secret after all? Was it bétter to say the same thing over and over and over again?

No doubt people were jealous of Mr. Rowland and he was open to base attacks by rivals. A certain Mr. Delcroix begins to advertise his Kalydor in *Martin Chuzzlewit*—in a number in which Mr. Rowland is also found—as being suited not merely to "female loveliness" but to "gentlemen who suffer from tenderness after shaving." Here is the chance of a very pretty quarrel, but Mr. Rowland seems to have thought it better to be discreet than valorous, whereupon Mr. Delcroix, after waiting for a little while to see what happens, goes one better and with unparalleled effrontery advertises Macassar Oil as well "imported under the sanction of the Lords of the Treasury for the use of Her Majesty and their Royal Highnesses the Prince of Wales and the Princess Royal." And then, when once again we are a-tiptoe expecting a terrific battle, nothing happens and there is no more Delcroix. Was it poison or a bravo's dagger? What befell him we shall never know.

There were others who could do wonders for the hair. There was Oldridge with his "Balm of Columbia," William Grimstone with his "Aromatic Regenerator," Unwin & Albert who made the "Columbia Hair Dye" and reinforced their works with a dear little picture of a bearded and particoloured gentleman, half of him Unwin'd and half of him un-Unwin'd. There was Dr. Locock's Lotion "for the growth of the hair", and this was prepared by Lea & Perrins, chemists of Worcester, who on

almost the next page advertised the Worcestershire
sauce with which we connect their name.   Rimmel
was ready with fragrant perfumes; so were Piesse &
Lubin, who sold a "Musical Nosegay, three melodies
in a pretty case 7s. 6d.—single sample 2s. 6d."   In
short there were various kind people prepared to
make hair shining and lustrous or to provide it
ready made for those who had not got it.   Waller
had a price list of hair plaits including the Frizzette,
the Alexandra Frizzette (here we see the influence
of the beautiful Princess of Wales), also All-Round
and Long Frizzettes.   Hubert with his Roseate

Powder was prepared to remove hair; under the
heading of "Beautiful Women" he said "The
Thorn that veils the Primrose from our view is
not more insidious to Nature than Superfluous Hair
on the Face Neck or Arms of Beauty."   There was
nobody to help wash hair or shave it off.   The
soap makers, afterwards so vociferous, were silent.
It is only in *Edwin Drood*, at the very end of Dickens's
life, that I came upon Pears' Transparent Shaving
Soap, next door, by an odd chance, to another great
firm of modern advertisers, Bryant & May, who
even then struck on the box.   Pears has a picture
of a most elegant young man in a low-necked shirt
and a bow tie, shaving such parts of his smirking

face as are not obscured by a luxurious growth of whisker, and over it are the familiar words

"RECOMMENDED BY THE FACULTY."

The young man is so very elegant that he probably stropped his razor on the Graduated Chinese Razor strop patronized by H.R.H. Prince Albert. I hope, too, since there is so little talk of washing, that when he first hopped out of bed he made use of the Collapsible Shower Bath provided by Mr. Burton, of Oxford Street, who took the inside of the back page of the whole set of *Dombey* for his advertisements.

The head, having been occasion-ally soaped and regularly made to shine, must be kept dry in case of rain and this is done by Messrs. Sangster with their silk and alpaca umbrellas on Fox's Paragon Frames from 16*s*. in silk and from 10*s*. 6*d*. in alpaca. Their umbrellas are remarkably light, and are sold at the same price as those made of whalebone, to which they are superior in every way. They seem  to be sheltering the little gentleman in the tall hat and the white waistcoat very satisfactorily, but where on such a day did he get his shadow? That seems rather mysterious.

The ladies of course would never go out on a day on which there was the least chance of rain. Those delicate creatures needed only parasols, and for them Messrs. Sangster "beg respectfully to inform the Nobility and Gentry that they are pre-pared to offer to their notice, under the name of the Persian, the most novel Parasol ever manu-factured in this country. These Parasols are made of a peculiar fabric, without any seam whatever, and are ornamented with Oriental patterns in the richest colours, warranted fast." No price is mentioned—not even "from." Clearly the ladies are first to be lured into the shop, and then when they see the lovely Oriental patterns they will pay anything. Umbrellas could, if necessary, be reinforced by the 'Cork respirator', which is particularly recommended to invalids and all who attend evening meetings or places of amusements. The "ease with which it could be applied or removed made it universally appreciated by ladies," but the picture is of a gentleman, and why in the world he wears so singular a cap I cannot say. His nose could be enveloped as well as his mouth for another two shillings.

Another thing remains to be done for the sleek head, and that is to portray it. This can be done by Mr. Mayall, of Regent Street, by means of a Daguerreotype portrait. Mr. Mayall's are not like other people's photographs. He has been practising the art ever since M. Daguerre discovered it in 1839 (this is in 1853), he has built glass houses for his purpose, and "in producing a really good Daguerreotype a combination of appliances and favourable circumstances are required, deprived of which the art sinks to the insignificance justly belonging to the many wretched abortions claiming the same nomenclature and to be seen in almost every street." There are coloured portraits as well as plain ones, costing from five to ten shillings extra, and a stereoscopic portrait with an instrument can be had for two guineas. The plain Daguerreotype, including a frame or morocco case, costs from 17s. for the smallest or oval size to £2 12s. 6d. for the fifth or largest.

Somewhere in the old pages of *Punch* there is a picture of an exquisite footman showing his photograph to the cook, and saying that it is a pretty thing, but that it is a pity that the yellow of the uniform comes out black. This difficulty had not been wholly overcome by Mr. Mayall, for he gives detailed suggestions for the clothes to be worn by his sitters. "Ladies are informed that dark silks and satins are best for dresses; shot silk, checked, striped or figured materials are also good, provided they be not too light. The colours to be avoided are white, light blue and pink; shawls, scarfs, mantles, and all flowing drapery adds to the beauty picture; the only dark material unsuited is black of the velvet. For gentlemen, black, figured, check, plaid or other fancy vests and neckerchiefs are preferable to white. For children, plaid, striped, red or figured dresses; hair in ringlets enhances the general effect."

Most of us still possess in some ancient album a plaid or striped little grandmother or a grandfather grasping an umbrella, with his tall hat reposing on a marble-topped table. There are also those family groups which Mr. Mayall could "arrange so as to form artistic pictures." Of all the advertisers he has perhaps built for himself the best monument, more enduring even than Morison's lion.

CHAPTER VIII

MR. MOSES

DICKENS in his numbers is, as has been said elsewhere, hard to come by. He is there one day and the next he is gone, sold to a lucky collector. The books are not to be read at leisure or all in their right order, but as fortune and some kind lender dictates. Consequently Mr. Moses, the greatest of all advertisers, came to me not in the chronological order of his achievements, and I have had to write about him piecemeal. I hope he is none the worse for that, and that I may be forgiven for not following Mr. Weller's rule, "Reg'lar rotation, as Jack Ketch said, when he tied the men up."

Well, then, Mr. Moses, poet, tailor, hatter, and hosier of the Minories and Aldgate, first swam into my ken in the third number of *Dombey and Son*, where he has the honour of making his bow in the company of Mrs. Pipchin, and might well have quoted, though he never did, "'Who's your tailor?' said Mr. Toots." From that time he is faithful to the Dombey and Son Advertiser until the end, and there may even have been moments when his poetry outside was better fun than the prose inside, for, blasphemous as it may appear, I do declare that Mr. Carker and his teeth and the Honourable Mrs. Skewton are sometimes very poor company. At any rate Mr. Moses is often very good company, and it is pleasant to know that the advertisement did him good. At least he says it did, for in the last number he announces that "so great has been the success which the proprietors have met, that they have had placed at their disposal an amount of capital which has enabled them greatly to extend their operations."

When he appears on the back of the third number he has not really got into his stride. His first poem is a little laboured in its humour. It is called " E. Moses and Son's lines to A. Bull" and begins

> "Don't marvel that dealers in garments and wool
>   Should attempt to address a few lines to a 'Bull';
> A brief explanation will show what we mean
>   And the drift of these verses will clearly be seen:
> The 'Bull' we address is the fam'd Mr. John
> Who long has had dealings with Moses and Son."

He then proceeds to address Mr. Bull at considerable length, but it is rather poor stuff with puns about hats being crowned with success and so on.

"Our trousers shall prove that our house is the star," he sings, but his verses prove nothing of the sort. Gradually, however, he warms to his work until at last, in the eighth number, his genius reaches what I take to be its highest pinnacle in a poem called "A Gentleman." No extracts can do it justice. It must be set out in full length.

> What is a gentleman? a fellow man
> Who tries to be as perfect as he can.
> A gentleman is one who has a mind
> For things respectable, and things refined.
> You'll know a gentleman by conversation
> And matters which pertain to education.
> A gentleman is civil and polite,
> Not often wrong, but very often right;
> A gentleman, in matters of the purse,
> Will make his fortune better—never worse.
> These various qualities go very far
> To make a man a gentlemanly star;
> Yet more's required—(dispute it, if you can.)
> To constitute a perfect gentleman,
> Manners and learning (you will all confess)
> Are nought without the supplement of dress;

Good dress in fact, will cover sore defects
While credit on the wearer it reflects.
Moses and Son are such as all admire
For articles in gentlemen's attire ;
A suit from Messrs. Moses' stylish mart
Respectable appearance can impart ;
The "beau ideal" which the mind supposes,
Is one who dresses in the clothes of Moses.
No slovenly appearance they impart,
But all is neat, though elegantly smart :
This is the reason why the gents repair
To Messrs. Moses' Warehouse—you know where ;
And on these grounds, have Messrs. Moses sought
The favour of respectable support.
Moses and Son (dispute it if you can)
Make all these articles on such a plan
As cannot fail to make—

A GENTLEMAN.

There are no doubt a few technical defects. Mr.
Moses was either rather lazy, or else showed a poverty
of invention in twice using that obvious tag "dispute it if you can" to rhyme with "gentleman",
and he should not have said in almost consecutive
lines that his garments could "impart" an appearance respectable and not slovenly. Still, who that
has put a "jam" or a "nunc" into an hexameter to
make it fit will throw a stone at him? and there are
many really beautiful lines, such as that about the
"matters of the purse." I do not think he had ever
climbed to such heights before or ever did so again,
but he was always capable of great moments.
Just as in the case of Dickens himself, there would
suddenly come a word or two of pure gold in the
midst of dross. There is for example the poem called
"My Choice," with a refrain to the effect that
Moses will ever be the poet's choice. I do not
think I am wrong in saying that it contains two
lines which raise the whole poem to a higher level :

I love a gentlemanly hat
Nor have I failed to meet with that.

There is a kind of heavenly flatness about those lines, which remind one of Wordsworth at his flattest, while it has just a touch of that poem beloved of sentimental audiences at smoking concerts, "The green eye of the little yellow god."

The gentlemanliness of Moses and Son is a theme constantly harped upon, as in Lord Chesterfield's advice to his son upon matters of dress.

> No hatters can equal the tradesmen I name,
> And their boots and their shoes have a very high claim,
> So I trust that you'll do as your father has done—
> Study fashion by dealing with Moses and Son.

"My Choice," "The Top of the Tree," and "Public Applause" all show the value of a haunting refrain at the end of each verse. They also enable Mr. Moses to deal with his coats, shirts, hats, boots and furs, each in a separate and striking manner. The last verse of "Public Applause" may serve as a specimen.

> E. Moses and Son in their Hosiery too,
> And in Outfits, as well, are believed to out-do,
> Moses' wonderful Warehouse (renown'd far and near)
> Is "the Public's own Pet"—What a splendid idea!
> And as all things are sold by Economy's laws,
> No wonder it meets with such "Public Applause."

In the second half of *Dombey* there comes first of all a poem to The London Stone, in which that venerable relic is apostrophized as to all the wonderful tales it could unfold. It had been there before St. Paul's; it had seen all manner of garments come and go, but had it ever seen such clothes as came from Aldgate? The poet firmly answers his own question.

> "No, antique Stone! there never was a day
> When Fashion showed us what she now discloses;
> And (could'st thou speak) in justice, thou would'st say
> I never saw such Dress as that of Moses."

After that flight the poet ceases for a while to seek casual inspirations and embarks on a series of poems on the seasons, Christmas, New-Year, Spring and so on, which are less exciting.

> Then haste to Moses' Mart and freely bring
> Your needful orders for the opening Spring
> While smiling flow'rets bloom and warblers sing.

There is an occasional outburst such as this, but for the most part he seems to be writing too definitely from his brief.   There is one novel departure when he gives us a parody on "The Ivy Green," the poem which the old clergyman at Dingley Dell recited when the Pickwickians first visited Manor Farm, no one knows why, unless it was that Dickens had failed to get it into a Magazine and did not want it wasted.   It is called "The Rival Mart," a slightly mysterious title, as it makes no allusion to any rival, but is entirely in praise of Mr. Moses's own mart.   It is very much on a par with the poem on which it is founded.

> Its shops are capacious, its show-rooms vast
>   To suit the business here—
> And Moses and Son have thus surpassed
>   All rivals far and near,
> Rising in a public part
> A rare good House in the Rival Mart.

Having enjoyed Mr. Moses so much in *Dombey* we give him a rapturous welcome when we find him again in *Bleak House*, but alas! he is scarcely the Moses that he was.   For one thing, he has been dethroned from the ample spaces of the back cover. That has been usurped by Mr. Heal and his lordly beds, and poor Moses has to put up with a beggarly inside.   And then he has become a mere prose labourer.   Only twice does he drop into poetry, and then some of the old sparkle and spirit have gone.

He begins this time, in ordinary small print, with "Anti-Bleak House," a fine purple patch describing a house where "the north winds meet to howl an ignoble concert, and bitter blasts mourn like tortured spirits of rebels, who, though prisoners, are unsubdued; where the whirlwind and the hurricane vow their vengeance; and the walls and timbers creak resistance, and, like wounded gladiators, rise again boldly to defy the antagonist." This is all very well, but he would have done better to quote Dickens himself, who could convey snugness indoors with a storm out of doors better than any one. Think once again of Tom Smart driving across Marlborough Downs with the vixenish mare and coming to the heavenly little inn, with the red light shining through the windows, and the fire piled half-way up the chimney! I need scarcely point out that "Anti-Bleak House" ends with the statement that "E. Moses and Son are perfectly satisfied of the resistance their dress will offer to wind and water."

Mr. Moses goes on to April showers and May flowers, and, inspired by Jarndyce and Jarndyce, has an elaborate joke about a suit in Chancery and a suit out of Chancery, the latter made of course at the famous Mart. Then suddenly in the fifth number he breaks fresh ground. He appeals no longer to the man who wants to look gentlemanly but to the emigrant who is going to rough it on a voyage to Australia in search of gold. The excitement over the gold rush may be traced in other advertisements about this time. The Gutta Percha Company, for example, launch out into a picture of the emigrant in a tail coat and whiskers packing a small wooden box. Outside the window is a sailing ship, while a life-buoy, rests cheerfully against the wall and he is cramming his box with guttapercha mugs and boots and buckets, all essential at the gold diggings. In *David Copperfield*, by the way,

L

there is a pleasing allusion to the emigrant in an advertisement of the Cork Floating Mattress and Boat Cushion. "The emigrants' Bolster is earnestly recommended to the notice of those whose means are too limited to purchase a mattress, as it is impossible that loss of life can happen at sea from wreck or fire, if every emigrant be provided with one of them."

In no less than eight numbers of *Bleak House* Mr. Moses devotes his remarks more or less to the emigrant, though it must be admitted that the clothing specified in his price lists will hardly be of much use to that hardy adventurer. If he buys a "fancy quilting vest" from "2*s*. 6*d*." to "7*s*. 6*d*." it can only be to preen himself when he returns home in triumph with his pockets full of what Mr. Moses calls "the needful."

In the fifth number the emigrant is appealed to under the alluring heading of "New Empire," with allusions to the Emperor Constantine, whose wealth Australia has far outstripped. In the sixth there are held out to him more definite promises. "It is rather a Bold Stroke when a Man whose earthly property, including a Wife and a very large Family, will not fetch more than Fifty Pounds, but firm in his resolution, and determined in his steps, he avows he will be possessed of Fifty Thousand Pounds. Yet such a Stroke is reasonable and safe enough if he procures a suitable and economical Outfit at E. Moses and Son's, and with that proceeds to Australia, the land for gold and wages."

The eighth number hints delicately that the emigrant may encounter some discomforts on the sea. "A change from a Landsman to a Sailor is sometimes rather a radical one", he is told, "particularly if the said person has not been to sea before: a thousand new feelings may arise in the neighbourhood of the digestive organs." However, three numbers later he has quite got over such unpleasant sensations; he is returning home having made his pile, and with proper gratitude rushes to Mr. Moses the source of all his good fortune, to be once more attired as a gent. He "employed the last few pounds of his patrimony in preparing for Australia. Procuring his outfit at E. Moses and Son he proceeded to the "Diggings," where his adventures and success were equally surprising, and having returned with abundance of the needful, has furnished a very affecting narrative for all classes. It is only justice to suppose, that the Establishment where he took the first step towards wealth should form a prominent part in his story."

Apart from the gold rush there is only one topical allusion in the series, and that is to Table Moving, which was presumably exciting people at the time. A year or two before *Bleak House* began America had been interested in "The Rochester Knockings" and the Fox Girls. Furniture had so persistently moved about in the neighbourhood of the famous Daniel Dunglass Home, then a boy of seventeen, that his aunt had first thrown a chair at him, then summoned a Wesleyan, an Independent and a Baptist minister to wrestle with him and, these proving futile, turned him out of doors. Mr. Moses does not treat the subject with altogether becoming gravity. He makes the kind of jokes about it that would have pleased old Mr. Wardle when in a Christmas mood at Manor Farm, for, says he, "Table-moving is a very interesting experiment, and very engaging too, some say it requires both sexes to manage it effectually and when their fingers are properly united." He adds of course, that there is no delusion about tables being turned at the Mart, where entire novelty has been introduced in cut and make.

I am so grateful to Mr. Moses that the least I can do is to mention one or two of his prices and, though they are all guardedly stated as being "from" a certain sum, they make the mouth water. If only our tailors to-day had half his complaint! In the last number of *Bleak House* we find that "Paletots" in every new material can be had from 10*s*. 6*d*. and "Lounging and Morning Coats" in holland from 3*s*. 6*d*. and in tweed, cashmere, alpaca and angola from a guinea, "The Dress Coat" corresponding presumably to "The Egg" of Dan Leno's old joke can be had from 17*s*. 6*d*., "super quality" £1 5*s*., and best quality £2 15*s*. Waistcoats begin at half a crown, and trousers, whether plain or fancy, at only a florin more. I feel inclined to rush to Aldgate murmuring softly to myself—

> If you entertain any respect for your calves,
> Come to Moses, whose articles ne'er rip in halves,
> Come to Moses, who drain not your purse to its dregs,
> To Moses, whose Trousers will honour THE LEGS.

After lamenting that Mr. Moses had fallen off from the poetry of *Dombey* to the prose of *Bleak House*, I found that I had done him a grave injustice; he had been writing poetry long before *Dombey*, for he had written it in *Martin Chuzzlewit*. He had not then come to the height of his powers and confined himself chiefly to prose; poetry was but a single outbreak or adventure. The advertisements in the Chuzzlewit Advertiser are not particularly exciting, and there are those long pamphlets as to the Corn Laws which, though interesting no doubt to the political student, are of a heart-breaking dullness to the ordinary person. So the reader is ploughing his way conscientiously through them when suddenly he gives the glad cry of a miner who has found a nugget. Here in the ninth number is a little pink pamphlet tidily sewn in at the end. It is called "The eighth wonder of the world," and inside—heavenly sur-prise!—is Mr. Moses.

He begins by enumerating the seven recognized

wonders of the world, and follows them by several possible candidates for the eighth place, "the great wall of China, St. Peter's at Rome, the fact of railway locomotion, and the Thames Tunnel.' But needless to remark there is something to be said against the claims of each one of these, and Moses's two establishments at Aldgate and the Minories "are alone worthy of the honour." Aldgate presents a "scene of grandeur and beauty never before equalled in commercial speculation." The Minories establishment, though "not quite so splendid," is yet "an object of great public admiration." Both of them have "gilded case compartments, marbled pillars and bronzed images on the landings," both "present the appearance of an extensive holiday fair," and Aldgate actually possesses, crowning what Mrs. Gamp would have called its "parapidge," the Royal Arms in stone as the climax and consummation of its gorgeousness. This pamphlet having been so successful, Mr. Moses in the next number conceives the luminous notion of translating his prose into verse and does it much as a schoolboy by pure brute force of dictionary and gradus translates some remarks upon spring into the requisite number of elegiac lines. Indeed, Mr. Moses all through his career has two distinct styles of verse. One is the "Mr. Wilkinson, a clergyman" style, setting forth with never a joke plain facts for plain people; the other is the brilliant and facetious style with those plays upon words which are intended to appeal to the more intellectual wearers of fancy vests and doeskin trousers. In this case he is in his serious mood and on his high horse.

> How can language justly tell
> Of scenes so indescribable?
> Struck with a building so sublime
> Your eye in wonderment will climb.
> Here at one view the eye explores
> A wide expanse of lofty doors.

Broad windows glazed with costly glass
And sashed with rods of solid brass.
And higher still the vision marches,
The eye is met with spreading arches,
Whose lofty height and wide expansion
Might well adorn a regal mansion.
Still higher on the building's face
A sculptured image you may trace.
And at the crown the eye is met
With an imposing parapet,
Supporting like a stately throne
The Royal Arms in massive stone.

And so on and on for a large number of lines dealing not merely with the building but all the clothes (which invariably rhyme with "those") inside it. This poem is repeated in the eleventh number, and then he is silent again for a while, leaving the field open to the other tailor, Mr. Doudney, who has lately moved westward and opened a shop in Bond Street to the virtues of which "ONE HUNDRED NOBLEMEN and a very large circle of the Haut Ton" have testified.

However, in the sixteenth number there is no Doudney (they seemed to have boxed and coxed), and there is Mr. Moses with a leaflet, yellow instead of pink, called "The Temple of Fashion." In that temple of Aldgate customers "can be conducted through the length and breadth of the Establishment by a person who has strict injunctions to make no allusion to the purchasing of articles, unless first questioned by the parties themselves." There follows the usual list of garments, of no great interest except in one small particular. Some light is thrown on the habit of getting mourning in a desperate hurry, which had formerly, as it seems, been considered unnecessary. "The melancholy suddenness with which our dearest ties are too often snapt asunder and the now almost general custom of going into mourning immediately subsequent to decease has induced E. Moses and Son to make such arrangement etc."

No sound critic will deny that Mr. Moses's art was still in its infancy at the time of *Chuzzlewit*, had greatly developed in *Dombey* and had somewhat fallen away in *Bleak House;* but it is at least arguable that it was not *Dombey* but *David Copperfield* in which he called himself the "minion of the million," that saw him at his zenith. For simple beauty, he may never again have written anything to equal "The Gentleman," but as regards wit and sparkle and the quite Hood-like splendour of his puns, he never in *Dombey* came up to "The Whale in the Thames," to be found in the sixth number of *Copperfield*. He has gained in self-confidence, he knows himself to be on intimate and familiar terms with his readers and so feels able to indulge in little asides to them and even to laugh slyly at himself.

The Whale in the Thames

The mighty monster captured in the Thames
May justly swell my advertising gems.
I call them "gems" not vainly, O dear no!
But "gems" will rhyme with Thames, and so and so.
The mighty whale no doubt be-wailed his lot,
When near the "Basin" of the Thames he got.
And doubtless he was not without amaze
When thus he "grazed" himself near "Kentish Grays."
But soon his captors told him woeful tales
By landing on the beach a "Prince of W(h)ales."
Be that which way it may, I beg to state,
I'm "fishing" after trade in this huge "bait."
When I, with thousands more, stood by to gaze
Upon the wand'ing whale, safe moored at Grays,
I thought of that "Leviathan" Depôt
Which raised a "swimming" trade twelve years ago.
Till Moses came, the trade was in a thrall
And "blubbering" monopoly ruled all.
But Moses' soon exposed his "oily" terms,
Exhibiting themselves the first of firms.
They brought the monster to his proper scale
And proved he "threw a sprat to catch a whale."
And now their purchasers appear to be

As plentiful as "fishes" in the sea.
Moses by merit "only fish for praise,"
And so I thought the other day at Grays
Where thousands met to see the fated fish—
To dress as beautiful as you could wish.
The guests, I mean, were clad.   Don't be mistaken,
I wish to save my grammar and my bacon."

His grammar is a little dim in places, and pedantic persons might say that a whale was not a fish, but still it is a fine effort. Mr. Moses thought so himself, for he reprints it in the next number, and Mr. Nicoll, who is occupying the back of the cover with his shop in Regent Street, is roused to retort with a capital picture. Whether it was Mr. Nicoll who had the "Leviathan Depôt" I do not know, but Mr. Moses certainly had some other shop in mind and returns several times to the attack against that "monopoly" which he had exposed.

Mr. Moses once or twice reverts about this time to his punning style, as in his remarks about the Dog-Days. It can hardly," he says, "be considered dog-grel when E. Moses and Son say

> Let the dog-days
> Be light tog-days.

He does not want to be dog-matical since he *embarked* in trade," and so on with all the jokes carefully underlined and in inverted commas. As to the rival mart, all Mr. Moses has to say about him is that his styles "be-Tray" him. Alas! there are no dogs called Tray nowadays. The last of them died with Trilby.

Here is a poem of the same period in which his rhyming is rather subtler and more ingenious than usual. It is called "So—So."

> Thousands to Moses' Warehouse press;
> And pray what makes them go so?
> Because the articles of dress
> Are anything but "So—So."

The dress is good, the dress is smart,
　　And all the buyers know so;
And not a thing at Moses' Mart
　　Is ever viewed as "So—So."

　*　　　*　　　*　　　*　　　*

Come then and swell the list of those
　　Who aid the vast Depôt so;
And purchase Moses' new Spring clothes
　　So opposite to "So—So."

If you, in point of dress, are one
　　That's called a virtuoso,
　Right pleased you'll be with M. & Son,
　　Whose dress is never "So—So."

There are also several poems in his less complex
manner such as that called "The Powder Headed
Gentleman." It is too long to quote in full and
begins by saying that people in general had completely given up powder.

Yet Mr. White, a man whom well I know,
Wore powder till a week or two ago.
Wear it he would in spite of what was said
Making a laugh of every other head.

However he changed his mind because he bought
a suit from Moses.

The cloth was elegant, the style "all right"
(To quote the homely phrase of Mr. White).

And the consequence was

That he began to fear that powdered hair
Would be a most destructive thing to wear;
He thought and thought till on that very day
His powder pride and prejudice gave way."

Observe the literary allusion in that last line, put
there for the select few who have heard of Miss
Austen and will chuckle to themselves with a sense

of superiority. Finally the poet, having nobly restrained himself, explodes in one last tremendous pun:

> I shall be proud indeed (and no one prouder)
> At swelling "Moses" train by means of powder.

In the March number he says

> When next upon this printed sheet
> The name of Moses' mart you meet
> My Muse will touch her trading lyre
> In praise of Moses' Spring Attire.

but the Muse does nothing of the sort and has only a rather mild poem on an old picture:

> Look at the coat how wretchedly it fits,
> And see the vest! how awkwardly it sits.

There is more spirit in the "Vaunting Marts of Rivalry" to the air of "The Flaunting Flag of Liberty."

> The vaunting marts of rivalry
>   Which none can well admire
> Shall never once be sought by me
>   In purchasing attire.
> The only warehouse which appears
>   To claim my zealous aid
> Is a mart that's brav'd for many years
>   The battle of the trade."

The verses "To Old Neptune" begin well:

> Come Father Neptune! I'm disposed to be
>   A little chatty for a certain reason.
> Thou knowest well, as monarch of the sea,
>   That this is what I'll term a "ducking season."

After that they fall off, and a far finer description of the pleasures of the seaside is to be found in prose. It is called "The Seaside Trip," and the

writer begins by saying how pleased he is with
himself because before he set out he bought various
garments at Aldgate. Then "on arriving at my
destination and mingling, as I did, with the *élite*
of the watering-place where I had chosen to stay,
I found that the fashion and make of *my* dress
was precisely the same as those of the principal
part of the visitors. E. Moses and Son, I found,
had been the Tailors selected by those parties who
knew well how to make a judicious selection in
such matters as those."

And now we must say adieu to Mr. Moses. Can
we do so better than when he is "a tip-toe as the
highest point of being," patronizing Dickens himself? This he does in his poem, "The Proper Field
for Copperfield," in which he says that if only all
his customers would buy the book it would have
"a wondrous circulation."

> It should bedeck the poor man's board
> And swell the volumes of my lord.
> This novel merits to be read
> Wherever Moses' fame has spread,
> Which like a banner is unfurled
> Throughout the habitable world.

CHAPTER IX

ANY chapter on clothes must necessarily be bereft of its brightest ornament because Mr. Moses and his beautiful poetry had to have one all to themselves.

There are other tailors, but none that are comparable to Moses, and only one who on a single occasion drops into poetry as a friend. Some learned student of ladies' fashions could possibly write a short illustrated history of the changes in them from the time of *Pickwick* to that of *Edwin Drood*, but I am incapable of it. All I can do is to set down casually some odds and ends that strike me as pleasant.

Observe, for example, the Caspiato or Folding Bonnet which, if by no means so constant as the Gentleman's Invisible Peruke, yet makes a fairly regular appearance. It also belongs, like the peruke, to the head, and a picture of the two will be found not inappropriately in that chapter. As in the case of the peruke the wearer could measure herself for it, and though made in a variety of styles it never cost more than one guinea. The pictures show how deftly it folded itself. "The Caspiato packs in a box two inches deep; and this portability is obtained without interfering with the appearance of the Bonnet, which is made of all materials, and may be trimmed in the highest fashion: it is not more expensive, and surpasses all Bonnets for elegance, convenience, and lightness."

The Caspiato was made by a gentleman called
Smith, whose fame has not otherwise reached me,
but turning over the page I come to the celebrated
name of Jay, with a picture of his shop in Regent
Street. It seems that up to this time Mr. Jay
was only interested in mourning. He was the
" London General Mourning Warehouse," and Mr.
Mould himself could not more delicately have
reminded families of what was expected of them
in their bereavements of more or less severity.
About 1855 so many ladies had asked him for
coloured millinery and mantles " when the period
for the use of mourning apparel shall have expired "
that he launched out into another establishment
under the direction of one Laure Vouillon. And
Mlle. Laure herself launched out into enthusiastic
French as to the " modes, fleurs, mantelets et nou-
veautés " which came every week from the most
fashionable Paris houses.

This new branch of the business, at No. 246
Regent Street " vis-à-vis Princes Street, Hanover
Square", seems to have flourished, for its advertisements grow larger and larger within the year
(not in French but in honest English), and the shop
took the name of " The Sponsalia." There is
something modern and go-ahead in the statements
that " the prices are marked in plain figures " and
that the visitor is "on no pretence importuned to
make a purchase."

The announcements of the General Mourning
Warehouse contain the names of various substances
that sound to me mysterious, Paramatta, Bombazine, Merino and Crape. I do know something
about Bombazine, however, for when the celebrated
Miss Mary Blandy was hanged she " suffered in a
black bombazine sack and a petticoat " and when
Mrs. Fitzadam, formerly Miss Hoggins, returned to
Cranford as a prosperous widow in rustling black
silks, Miss Jenkyns declared that "bombazine would

have shown a deeper sense of her loss." Silk,
according to Mr. Jay, was suitable for "slight or
complementary mourning." I find no mention of
black satin in this advertisement (which I take
from October, 1846), although Mrs. Manning had
not then elected to be executed in it. It was just

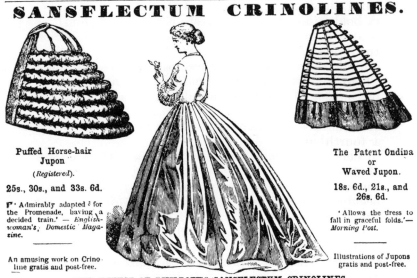
three years later that this redoubtable murderess
was hanged in front of Horsemonger Lane Gaol,
dressed in a black satin dress trimmed with black
lace and a black veil. Dickens wrote a letter to
The Times, in which he denounced the horror of a
public execution and the ribald conduct of the crowd;
and black satin earned a lasting unpopularity.

There are various other shops making various garments for ladies, but they nearly all lack fire and originality, though I must put in a good word for Mr. Hobson, of Lombard Street, who became more genteel and opened a shop in Regent Street. There is a *je ne sais quoi* about his lady in a riding habit which appeals to me. I have also found in *Our Mutual Friend* (1864) the makings of an agreeable squabble about crinolines. In the third number Mr. Philpott, of Piccadilly, announces in bold letters the "Sansflectum Crinoline." There is one picture of the Sansflectum Jupon which the *Court Journal* had declared "a most graceful crinoline, admirably adapted for the promenade." There is another of the "Ondina or Waved Jupon" by means of which a lady "may ascend a steep stair, lean against a table, throw herself into an arm chair, pass to her stall at the Opera, or occupy a fourth seat in a carriage, without inconvenience to herself or others, or provoking the rude remarks of the observers." This blessed state of things "modifies in an important degree, all those peculiarities tending to destroy the modesty of Englishwomen."

In the next number Mr. Philpott is still advertising both the Sansflectum and the Ondina, but he is not left in sole possession, for a black-vizarded ruffian called Hubbell, of Fountains Court, in Aldermanbury, has the audacity to steal the beautiful and onomatopoeic title of Ondina, and apply it to a jupon of his own. What happened can only be guessed. It may be assumed that Philpott threatened Hubbell, and that the upstart of Aldermanbury was for a while crushed; but suddenly in the nineteenth number he reappears having dropped the Ondina but proffering the Gemma and the Sansflectum Crinoline,—as bad a business as that of the man who was not Rowland and yet made Kalydor and Macassar Oil. And then there

is no Philpott. Had he in turn been crushed or had
he unsuspectingly left the field, believing Hubbell
to be extinct? It is the last number. Silence falls
upon the battlefield of the crinolines, and I know
no more.

It may have been a three-cornered fight, for there
were other makers. There were also in *Our Mutual
Friend* Messrs. Thomson, who disguised their advertisement so skilfully that you had to read at least
half of it before you discovered what they were driving
at. They began with a disquisition on Shakespeare
and a pilgrimage to his birthplace in honour of his
tercentenary. Shakespeare still remained supreme,
but "in manners and morals it required centuries
to produce a revolution as complete as that effected
by the poet in the expression of thought; while
the no less important reform in the habiliments
wherewith we clothe the human form divine is
still an open subject for the pen of a modern
Shakespeare." In short what was wanted was a
gentleman who "with burning words and sparkling
epigrams" should contrast "the symmetrical form
and graceful outline of the lady who wears Thomson's
prize medal watch-spring crinoline with the beauty
who renders herself as unlovely as possible by balloon
or barrel-like disfigurements."

To find this new Shakespeare, Messrs. Thomson gave
a hundred guineas for the best poetic compositions
written by the poets of 1864, and these were soon
to be offered to the public in a pamphlet. There
were two pictures, Queen Elizabeth in the costume
of her time and The Queen of Beauty in the most
graceful costume of 1864. What that costume was
Messrs. Thomson with artistic reticence refrained
from saying, but the winning poet probably guessed
right.

Now for the gentlemen, and first among the tailors,
though a long way after Moses, comes Mr. Edmiston,
of 69 Strand, opposite the Adelphi Theatre. His

YOUTH.—120, REGENT STREET.

PARENTS and GUARDIANS are respectfully invited to inspect the cost of the several garments here submitted, and considered necessary for the Universities, Public and Private Schools, &c. In this branch clever and efficient persons are employed by Messrs. NICOLL, as in all other departments, the result being the production of a more graceful and elegant appearance in Youths' Clothing than has hitherto been approached; while, at the same time, their durability and general excellence will be as strongly characterised as in NICOLL'S PALETOT.

VIEW OF CALCUTT

Where Messrs. D WILSON & Co. are the Sole Agents for H. J. and D. NICOLL, of 114, 116, 118, and 120, Regent Street, and 22, Cornhill, London, and Cloth Manufacturers.

Merchant Clothiers, Paletot Patentees. Many use the word "PALETOT," but Messrs NICOLL are the Sole Patentees of the design and material used in the graceful and inexpensive article of gentlemanly attire.

118, Regent Street, is a Department for Robes, College Gowns, &c.

116, Regent Street, is a Department for Military and Diplomatic Uniforms, &c.

114, Regent Street, is a Department for Paletot and Novelties in Costume.

22, Cornhill, is the City Depôt for Specimens of each of the above Departments.

BRADBURY AND EVANS, PRINTERS, WHITEFRIARS.

EDMISTON'S
CRIMEAN OUTFIT,
£18 18s.

Comprising the following requisites for Officers proceeding to the seat of War, viz.:—

Waterproof Cape and Hood.
    ,,   Camp Boots.
    .,   Ground Sheet.
Folding Bedstead.
Mattrass and Pair of Blankets.
Canteen for Two Persons.
Sponging Bath.

Bucket and Bason.
Brush Case.
Lantern.
Havresack.
Pair of Pack Saddle Trunks, with Straps and Slinging Irons complete.

Attention is respectfully invited to

EDMISTON'S WATERPROOF WINTER CAPE, WITH HOOD,
CAMEL-HAIR LINED.

PAIR of BULLOCK TRUNKS, forming BEDSTEAD,
With Straps and Slinging Irons, complete in one, £6 10s.

PORTABLE WATERPROOF PATROL TENTS,
Weighing 10 lb., price £2 2s.

PORTABLE INDIA-RUBBER BOATS,
On View, same as used in the Harbour of Balaklava.

THE POCKET SIPHONIA,
OR WATERPROOF OVERCOAT,

Weighing 10 oz. Price, according to size, 40s. to 50s. ; all silk throughout, 50s. to 60s.

Stout Siphonias, 25s. to 35s. Overalls, 10s. 6d. Yacht Jackets, 18s. 6d.
Reversible Alpacas, 35s. each, suitable for Clergymen.

NOTICE.—NAME & ADDRESS STAMPED INSIDE. NONE OTHERS ARE GENUINE.

EDMISTON & SON, No. 69, STRAND, LONDON.

strong point was the protecting of his customers against the weather. He was the maker of the Pocket Siphonia, or waterproof overcoat, which could be "easily folded to carry in the pocket or on the saddle." He added "the important feature of this waterproofing is being mineralized, which effectually resists the powerful heat of the sun and the most violent rains, also obviating the stickiness and unpleasant smell peculiar to other waterproofs." His two pictures here presented must have highly incensed Mr. Sangster the maker of umbrellas. I cannot help thinking however that the gentleman portrayed *did* want an umbrella, for his tall hat must have suffered sadly.

When I first saw that picture my mind instantly flew off at a tangent to *Frank Fairlegh*. I hope some of my readers may remember the scene in that beloved book, in which Mr. George Lawless puts on a new waterproof coat and the Rev. Mr. Mildman, the tutor, believes him to be disguising himself in a carter's smock frock in order to visit a scene of vulgar dissipation. The tailor said of the coat that it was "a new invention—a man named Macintosh hit upon it." This sent me to my *Dictionary of National Biography*, to see if Frank Fairlegh was accurate as to his dates. Smedley was a private pupil with Dr. Millet at Brighton in 1834–5. Macintosh first took out a patent in 1823, but encountered many difficulties and made slow progress. In 1836 he brought an action for the infringement of his patent against a silk mercer; the trial excited much interest and eminent scientific men gave evidence. Perhaps Smedley, in looking back, confused the date of this trial with that of the original introduction of the coat, and perhaps he did not, and it does not very much matter.

The Pocket Siphonia was not Mr. Edmiston's only claim to fame. He invented the Versatio, or

Reversible Coat, which served "the double purpose of forming two in one without trouble, one side presenting a gentlemanly morning coat, the other side a riding, shooting or hunting coat, in any texture or colour desired." It was "worthy the attention of the nobleman, merchant or trades- man." On the left in the picture we behold, as I suppose, the nobleman, but no coat can alter him; he looks equally noble whether he wears it inside out or outside in. Not so the gentleman on the right. At one moment he is the prosperous merchant smoking the cigar, which marks his opulence. The next he reverses his coat, flings away his hat, seizes his gun, and, except for his legs, he looks almost a nobleman about to shoot over his lordly estate. "These varying properties the public must recognise as an union of novelty and usefulness not hitherto accomplished." Either the nobleman or the mer- chant could, by the way, shoot with Eley's Patent Wire Cartridges, which were advertised in *Nickleby* with an extract from a letter of the famous Colonel Hawker praising them. Colonel Hawker also recom- mended to him John Chapman's gloves for Partridge Shooting.

When the Crimean War broke out it gave Mr. Edmiston his chance, and for eighteen guineas˙ he provided an outfit for officers proceeding to the seat of war including waterproof, cape, and hood, camp boots, and ground sheet, bedstead, blankets, bucket, basin, lantern, haversack and sponging bath. The gentleman in the picture with the fixed bayonet is wearing several of these things and a pocket Siphonia into the bargain. Mr. Edmiston could also provide portable india-rubber boats as used in the harbour of Balaklava. In more peaceful times he also made cricketing gloves, goloshes, ladies' capes and the "newly invented swimming gloves", though why anyone should want gloves to swim in goodness only knows.

Hair-Working Table.

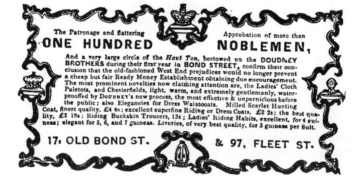

Other tailors made other garments with other
names. There was the "Patent Royal Albert Elastic
Cravat as a scientific invention"; Poulson made
the Par dessus and the Passe Partout; Barber, of
Cornhill, having had a classical education, made the
Anthropos coat as well as the Omega shirt; Powell,
of New Bond Street, made Comprimo Braces and
Templar caps for "sleeping, travelling or the soirée";
W. R. Whitelock sold Fashionable Rich Embroidered
Stocks for full dress, Rich figured Satin Scarves and
German cravats and Samuel Brothers called their
very splendid trousers the Sydenham, presumably
in honour of the Crystal Palace. Doudney, of
Lombard Street, who was a printer as well as a
tailor and advertized "the cheapest house for fancy
printing", despised fanciful names but was the first
man to invent the war cry "Save your income
tax." He also invented the Doudney Spring by
which Trouser Straps were to be superseded. He
became Doudney, of Bond Street, and was rewarded
by having one hundred noblemen, in capital letters,
as his customers. He had the poem in *Pickwick*,
already quoted, but was rather a dumb dog afterwards; his pictures, however, were not without merit.
There are two in *Martin Chuzzlewit*, one of a gentleman
with an eyeglass vaguely suggesting D'Orsay, and
the other consisting of soldiers, sailors, carriages and
horsemen, all interwoven rather in the manner of the
front covers of the Dickens numbers, and interspersed
with remarks in such small print that I cannot read
them.

Mr. Nicoll, of Regent Street, who regularly
occupied the outside of the back cover of *David
Copperfield*, had a somewhat similar composite picture of gentlemen riding, coaching, promenading
in assembly rooms and shooting attired, as it appears,
in turbans and kilts. I cannot help thinking that
somebody laughed at him about that picture, or
perhaps he only said to himself, " Excelsior." At

any rate he launched out into a scheme of advertising distinctly modern and ahead of his time. He produced a series of pictures having nothing in the world to do with coats or trousers but agreeable in themselves and calculated indirectly to please the customer. They represented a very catholic choice—San Francisco, the Cape of Good Hope, Calcutta, Edinburgh, Dublin, Carrickfergus Castle and Belfast Loch. They were quite well drawn and not in the least ridiculous. It was an indirect method of appeal which has become popular since but seems to have been new then.

Several people invented shirts including a gentleman in Leicester Square with the familiar name of R. Kipling, but most of them are merely shirts and there is an end of them. I do however feel some tenderness towards the Surplice Shirt made by John Sampson and Co., of Oxford Street, not for its own sake but for its pictures. Many of the gentlemen in these advertisements have luxuriant whiskers, but none of them can rival this one for "a growth of veeds of an alarmin' and sangvinary natur" as Sam Weller said of Mr. Smangle.

REGENT St. H. J. & D. NICOLL OR THE HILL

DUBLINE

Agent, Mr. GEORGE MACDONA, Molesworth Street, Dublin.

BRADBURY AND EVANS PRINTERS, WHITEFRIARS.

CHAPTER X

THE PILL

SOAP, chocolate, tobacco, mustard—all these have in later years proclaimed their virtues aloud and spent their millions in doing so. They have rivalled, if they have not dethroned, that great advertiser, the harmless necessary pill. But the pill had come into its kingdom when they languished in obscurity. When Dickens's books were coming out there was little talk of washing or munching, and less of smoking, but the pill was curing people of every known disease to the tune of many pages a month, and those old numbers bring us home to the glory that was Morison and the grandeur that was Holloway.

In the sixth number of *Little Dorrit* there appears a full page picture of the Morisonian Monument which was "erected in front of the British College of Health, New Road, London on the 31st of March (Day of Peace) A.D. 1856." The monument takes the form of a lion, with an expression of countenance which seems to say that if the pill does not do him good he will know the reason why. On the plinth is inscribed, "This memorial raised by a penny subscription has been erected A.D. 1856 to James Morison the Hygeist." Both Morison and Holloway appear in the *Dictionary of National Biography* (if there are other pill makers there I beg their pardons), and Holloway occupies the more space of the two. He made, as I imagine, more money, he built a College and a Sanatorium,

and made a collection of pictures but, as far as
I know, he never had a lion put up all to himself,
and so I still stick to Morison who came first and
had certainly the most engaging advertisements.
Morison was a Scot: he was born in 1770, and died
in 1840, so that he only got his lion sixteen years
after his death. He was a merchant at Riga and
in the West Indies, came home owing to ill health,
and settled at Bordeaux about 1814. Eight years
after that he cured himself by taking vegetable
pills at night and drinking lemonade in the morning,
and in 1825 he gave his remedy to the world. He
called himself the Hygeist, his shop the British
College of Health, and his remedy the "vegetable
universal medicine," though a coarse world would
call it Morison's pills. He fulminated against
doctors because they employed poisons, and he
would not let chemists sell his pills, but had an
agent of his own in every town and village. Some
of them by the way, seem to have done very well,
for in *Dombey* there is a picture of a gorgeous piece
of plate, of the value of £200, presented to a
Hygeist agent who had retired to keep an hotel.
The inscription describes the contributors as "48,000
advocates for the medical liberty of the subject
and enemies to persecution."

Occasionally the agents were wicked and swindled
Mr. Morison. In one number of *David Copperfield*
a J.P. and Notary Public from the Island of Cape
Breton, in Nova Scotia, writes pathetically to say
that there is a famine of pills in the South Eastern
section of the island owing to the treatment that
Mr. Morison has received from defaulting agents.
"I am requested," he says, "by a large and influential body of people personally known to me to
request you not to visit the sins of a few on a
grateful population."

One Morisonian agent was a woman, Miss Harriet
Beanham, of Crewkerne, agent for Somerset and

THE
MORISONIAN MONUMENT
ERECTED IN FRONT OF THE
BRITISH COLLEGE OF HEALTH, NEW ROAD,
LONDON,
ON THE 31st OF MARCH, (DAY OF PEACE,)
A. D. 1856.

THIS MEMORIAL,

RAISED BY A PENNY SUBSCRIPTION,

HAS BEEN ERECTED A.D. 1856.

TO

JAMES MORISON,

THE HYGEIST.

MORISON
Was the first to Protest against Bleeding, and the Use of Poisons in Medicine.

(EL OVER)

PIECE OF PLATE, VALUE £200, PRESENTED TO Mr. JOSEPH WEBB,
(HYGEIAN AGENT TO THE BRITISH COLLEGE OF HEALTH,) OF YORK, BUT
NOW OF THE BELL HOTEL, SCARBOROUGH, YORKSHIRE.

MANUFACTURED BY Messrs. RUNDELL AND BRIDGE, LUDGATE HILL, LONDON.

To Mr JOSEPH WEBB, of YORK,

This Epergne is presented
BY CONTRIBUTION,
From upwards of 48,000 advocates
For the Medical Liberty of the Subject and
ENEMIES TO PERSECUTION,
This 12th day of January, 1835.

The BRITISH COLLEGE OF HEALTH feel much pleasure in informing Hygeists that JOSEPH WEBB and his
family are in the enjoyment of excellent health. In a letter lately received from that worthy man, he says,
" I hope to keep it (the piece of plate) as long as I live, then to go down as an heir-loom to my family."

Dorset. She was afraid lest she should be thought forward and unladylike and explained her position at length in a letter to Mr. Morison. "It might justly appear extraordinary that such an appointment should be conferred on a female. To many it might seem like presumptuous arrogance and a love of notoriety, while by others a desire of profit may be assigned as the reason. I feel it then a duty to myself, to you, and to the Cause I advocate to state why I, an unprotected woman, leaving my native retirement and home, thus boldly, as it might seem, come forward and place myself so conspicuously before the public." She goes on to explain that the reason is the miraculous cure in her own case. "All my sisters, six in number, had, after equal sufferings with myself, been laid in their tombs in the bloom of life." Harriet alone was saved by pills and felt bound to testify accordingly.

Many of the Morisonian advertisements in the Dickens books must, owing to the dates, have come not from the Hygeist himself but from his successors. In *Nicholas Nickleby* however, he was still in full swing abusing the doctors, curing Miss Harriet, and looking forward to still greater triumphs. "Although," he says in 1838, "the Hygeian treatment has not yet to boast of any case of cure of Hydrophobia, nevertheless Mr. Morison, the Hygeist, has a strong conviction that it would be successful if properly persevered in." It was in the same year that, as recorded in *Bell's Messenger*, "A petition signed by upwards of 10,000 people was presented in the House of Commons by Mr. Hall, the Member for Marylebone, on Tuesday evening praying that a Committee be appointed to inquire into the merits of Hygeism. The petition was ordered to lie on the table."

After Morison's death the advertisements abated nothing of their quality. Indeed they grew more eloquent. Some were, like the Doctor in *Pickwick*,

"wery fierce." Just about the time of the presen-
tation of the epergne a young lady called Miss
Collier had died of an overdose of prussic acid, and
her doctor, who was a German and not an English
M.D., was tried and acquitted. "If," said the
Hygeists bitterly, "he had paid the fees to English
professors, there can be no doubt that the affair
would have been hushed up." They further observed, with three exclamation marks, that, "the
difference between the wilful poisoner and the
doctor is only a question of a few grains or drops,"
and a gentleman called "A looker on" cheerfully
prophesied that "Many victims to poison will fall
in consequence of that verdict."

The case of the Rev. Mr. Hewlett gave an opportunity for a violent onslaught. Mr. Hewlett was
a poor clergyman with an enormous family, and
in the teeth of the medical profession he treated
and cured them all with Morison's Pills. "What
must clergymen like Mr. Hewlett, and other
members of the Church who have such un-
bounded faith in the Hygeian System, think of
this precious manœuvre to prop up the false
and interested theory of Doctors? Surely there
is a God? And as surely will there be a day
of Judgment!"

Another blow to the doctors was the case of
the farmer who was told that he must certainly
die from ossification of the heart; one kind doctor
even lent him a book where he could read all about
it. "In a state of utter despair he heard of
Morison's Pills and commenced with them in small
doses; he felt their beneficial effect almost immediately at the seat of the disease. Notwithstanding
his wife said, 'My dear, you hear the pills kill
people; do give them up.' But as he was left
to die by the doctors he said 'he could but die
by the pills.' He continued to take them in large
and small doses and, instead of death, is restored

From the Original, in the Possession of
the British College of Health, London.

Portrait of a Horse

PRESENTED BY SIR RICHARD SUTTON, Bart.

TO THE HYGEIAN AGENT FOR THE COUNTIES OF DERBY, LINCOLN, AND LEICESTER,

IN CONSEQUENCE OF THE EXTRAORDINARY CURE OF MASTER HENRY SUTTON,

EFFECTED SOLELY BY THE USE OF 'MORISON'S UNIVERSAL MEDICINE,'

OF THE BRITISH COLLEGE OF HEALTH, LONDON.

Read the Case of Master Sutton, to be had, Gratis, of all the Hygeian Agents.

to good health and although in his 67th year, regrets that he has given up his farm."

The beauty of Morison's pills seems to have been that the more you took the better you were. They were infallible, so long as you did not, in Mr. Bob Sawyer's words about hot punch, "Fall into the vulgar error of not taking enough." A little matter of six or eight was recommended for smallpox, epilepsy or apoplexy, but a grateful patient who gave his experiences in *Bleak House* thought nothing of such miserable doses. He began quietly by taking five of No. 2 pill a day, and then increased the dose to nine. As this did him good he bought some No. 1 as well, and took a dozen of No. 1 on one day, and a dozen of No. 2 on the next. He began this course in January and stuck to it till May when he found that, far from being better, he was worse. He determined on an intensive campaign and went up to sixteen. Terrific symptoms followed, and up he went to eighteen a day. Still he got worse but he was not downhearted; he went up to twenty. The results cannot here be set down, though the hero himself did so at some length. Briefly, he grew worse again, but his faith was not shaken. "I took ten more," he says and then—well, I have not the pen of Mr. Rudyard Kipling in *My Sunday at Home*; it must be enough to say that something "went snap" in his inside, and he was suddenly and miraculously healed.

The Hygeist agent who was given the epergne was not the only one to be rewarded by grateful patients, and in 1847 we find a full page picture of a piebald horse, with a peevish expression of countenance and a wooded background, which was presented by Sir Richard Sutton to the agent for Derbyshire, Lincolnshire, and Leicestershire, "in consequence of the extraordinary cure of Master Henry Sutton, effected solely by the use of ' Morison's

Universal Medicine,'" Master Henry tempts us
down an agreeable by-path of history. His father,
a famous sportsman of his day, was a great friend
of the Squire, George Osbaldeston, and his mother
had come near to being Mrs. Osbaldeston instead
of Lady Sutton. The Squire tells us about it in
his autobiography. The lady was a beautiful Miss
Burton, and lived at Lincoln when Osbaldeston
also lived there as Master of the Burton: he was
disposed to fall in love with her, and her mother
encouraged the match, but, says the Squire, "despite the beauty of the young lady there was such
a lack of animation both in her countenance and
demeanour that my interest waned instead of
increasing. . . . Destiny had better fortune in
store for the young lady than marriage with myself;
a few years after she married Sir Richard Sutton
(a lad about fourteen at the time of which I write)
by whom she had nine or ten children. She did
not live very long, dying when she was thirty-five
or thereabouts." No doubt Master Henry Sutton
had been patted on the head by the "best sportsman of any age or county," who was privately
congratulating himself on not having married Miss
Burton and had all those tiresome children.

At the date of the Morisonian Monument there
was a gentleman called Fraser, a Hygeist Agent
in Edinburgh, who wrote several pages of small
print to explain why Morison deserved it, but he
was a dull dog, and the one faintly entertaining
thing he said was that no doctors could have monu-
ments because the highest medical authorities
themselves "admitted that it was questionable
whether their system had not done more real harm
than good to the world."

Mr. Fraser was dull, but he was no duller than
several other gentlemen who talked about pills.
There was Mr. Norton who made his Camomile
Pills "On philosophic principles." He produced

three solid pages of most uninviting aspect, with scarcely so much as a new paragraph to break the monotony. One joke or something like one he did make when he remarked that "the longer this medicine is taken the less will it be wanted," but I am afraid he did not mean it. Then there was The American Sugar-Coated Pill, which is to be found in one or two grand pill numbers of *Little Dorrit* together with Morison and Norton. Its owners could produce nothing better than a number of smudgy little testimonials, except once when they remarked that "its administration to the junior members of the family resembles the giving out of bonbons and comfits rather than that of a nauseous and disagreeable medicine." Here surely was a chance for a picture making a domestic appeal—a cosy room with firelight and a cat and a kettle hissing and a whiskered papa and children in best sashes prancing for pills; but this heaven-sent opportunity was missed. It is all so tedious and unimaginative that we sympathize with Du Barry's Revalenta, which shouts in its largest capitals in the same number "No more Pills!"

There is more to be said for "The Poor Man's Pill" advertised in *Nicholas Nickleby* with a large picture of the Apothecaries' Hall. "These Pills, now for the first time offered to the Public, have for years been extensively prescribed in private practice by a physician of great eminence and experience. It were to be regretted for the benefit of humanity that a medicine possessing such valuable properties should have remained so long a secret and could be procured at a pecuniary sacrifice so considerable as to render it available only to the wealthy classes. Through the exercise of extraordinary interest the original recipe has been procured."

John Kaye, Esq., of Dalton Hall, near Huddersfield, who made Worsdell's Vegetable Restorative

pills, also has his "moments of glad grace."
Malicious people might say as Mr. Squeers said of
Dotheboys Hall, "The fact is it ain't a hall", but
at any rate he had a coat of arms which perceptibly
cheered up the page. A very good coat of arms
it looks, with nothing too obviously professional
about it, unless the amorphous objects of vaguely
botanical appearance are meant for restorative
vegetables. The motto, however, is a sad come-
down—"Health and Happiness." I shall never
believe Mr. Kaye got that from the Heralds' College.
He had at least one pleasant testimonial as to
a lady who lived at Quick-hedge, near Mossley.
After a cataclysmic experience she was so much
better that "her husband said he was better pleased
than if he had received a present of twenty pounds."
There came a cheering phrase now and then, such
as that about Jemima Wheelhouse, of Wapping,
Bradford, who was "so afflicted with scurvy as
to be quite an object of pity," but usually the
testimonials did not rise above a rather squalid
level. In July of 1852, however, the coming of a
General Election inspired him to one of those
masterpieces of playing upon words of which
we may still see plenty of examples to-day,
as when a General asks us to *pay attention*
while he tells us how a certain soap or razor gives
a *uniform* shave. He begins on a lofty note,
"Fellow countrymen, in a short time you will be
involved in all the bustle of a GENERAL ELEC-
TION. Although the limits of the franchise will
leave the great majority of you in the position
of spectators rather than actors in the GREAT
NATIONAL DRAMA: yet it will be impossible for
any man of patriotic feelings to avoid being drawn
within the vortex of excitement." This stirring
beginning leads up to the statement that over-
excitement of the mind produces illness and that
all parties must prepare themselves for the struggle

by cooling their system and so composing the mind
and "nerving the whole man to patriotic action."

There follows his great moment of punning. "I
call upon *Ministerialists* to minister to their own
comfort as the best means of enabling them to
consult the nation's welfare; upon *Oppositionists* to
remove all obstructions in their own system; upon
Protectionists to protect themselves from the numerous liabilities of disease; upon *Free Traders* to keep
open the grand human passage as well as 'the
highway of nations'; upon *Conservatives* to con-
serve all that makes life valuable and society
happy; and upon *Radical Reformers* to strike at
the roots of evil in themselves. Whatever differences there may be on other points, all are agreed
that REFORM, end where it may, should BEGIN
AT HOME."

On the point of how these ends are to be accomplished there is "universal suffrage" and "Every man,
woman and child has a vote, which needs no ballot
to protect it from bribery or intimidation." Mr.
Kaye is like Mr. Jingle; he "don't presume to dic-
tate," but he ventures to suggest his PILLS "which,
without provoking external War, have never failed
to put down the most menacing INTERNAL DIS-
ORDERS."

Mr. Holloway had at this time hardly begun his
victorious career, and his advertisements are few
and uninteresting except for one screech of triumph:
"Amputation again prevented by Holloway's Oint-
ment." Mr. Parr is as a rule merely vociferous
and persistent about his Life Pills, but he rises once
above mediocrity. He suggests rather than asserts
that if you take enough of his pills you may live as
long as did the famous Old Parr, the oldest man in
the world. He begins by saying that "At present
the popular opinion is that the natural duration
of life is 70 years; but this is contrary to both sacred
and profane history. The opinion is no doubt

o

founded on a misunderstanding of the passage in the 90th Psalm" as to three score years and ten. "Now it must be remembered", he goes on, "that this Psalm is ascribed to Moses, and that he is not speaking of the lives of the men in general, but of what was occurring among the Israelites in the wilderness. They died not a natural death, but

were cut off for their sin and unbelief by judicial dispensations." A certain Dr. Farre maintained 120 to be the real span of life and quoted the sixth chapter of Genesis and the third verse: "My spirit shall not always strive with man for that he also is flesh; yet his days shall be an hundred and twenty years." Of course if anything can prove Dr. Farre

to be right it will be the taking of enough Life Pills.

Thus shall their humble labours merit praise
And future Parrs be blest with honour'd days.

The only pill-maker who can really hold his head up in Morison's company is one Ali Ahmed, who suddenly breaks out in the fourteenth number of *Bleak House* with a neat little green pamphlet headed by hieroglyphics, which I take to be Arabic. Ali Ahmed was of noble Persian descent, but was driven from his native country and fled to Aleppo where he flourished "between the years of the Herah 420-488," and if I ought to know when that was I don't. He discovered wonderful secrets and confided them on his death-bed to his family, and these secrets remained with his descendants until an "excellent and philanthropic Englishman" found them out, and thought it his bounden duty to introduce them at home. They were so famous in Aleppo that instead of saying that a man ran as if the devil was after him, people said he "ran as though he were running for the celebrated cough pills." There was also a little poem about him which might roughly be translated (without scanning very well):

"Men of all ages, fourscore years or nigh,
Run to the mart old Ali Ahmed's Pills to buy."

To add verisimilitude there are some lovely Arabic curly-wiggles which represent the original of this gem. So at least I gather, but the reader feels a little like poor M. Jourdain when he was made a Mamamouchi. "Ambousakin oqui boraf, Jourdain, salamalequi", said Cleonte. "C'est à dire", added Covielle, "Monsieur Jourdain, votre cœur soit toute l'année come un rosier fleury. Ce sont façons de parler obligeantes de ce pais-la."

In case anybody should be so base as to doubt the curly-wiggles, there is a letter from a gentleman in Damascus, and another from a gentleman in Bangkok, narrating how Prince Choo Fan of Siam was cured of a cough by Ahmed's pills, though his resident American physician had unsparingly dosed him in vain.

Furthermore—and this really must convince the most sceptical—the proprietors have secured a cast from an old bust of the "celebrated and good man," and have commissioned a gifted artist "whose magic touch has reproduced a living resemblance of Ali Ahmed." This can be seen at the depôt, where the "Treasures of the Desert" can likewise be procured in boxes from 1s. 1½d. to 10s. 6d. "silver-gilt in the Oriental style."

I like to think that somewhere in a niche in some suburban home there stands a treasured bust of Socrates or Mr. Gladstone, which had once been Ali Ahmed.

CHAPTER XI

VIXERE fortes ante Agamemnona—there were great beggars before Lord Knutsford, though not quite such great ones, and the London Hospital was begging in the Our Mutual Friend Advertiser in 1864. Under the title of "Epidemic of Typhus Fever" the Committee pointed out that "The London Hospital is the only Institution in the Metropolis for the treatment of Contagious Fevers and for the protection of the public from the spread of Contagion. It differs from almost all other Hospitals in conferring direct benefits upon all classes of the community—upon the rich, as well as upon the poor. It is capable of accommodating 260 patients."

That appeal seemed an old friend that deserved a place, but into what chapter would it go? It occurred to me that there must be a miscellaneous chapter devoted to old friends, people who were advertising in Dickens's day, and are still advertising now so that, as we read their names, we feel inclined to exclaim sentimentally, "Dear me! to think of that! It quite reminds me of new times." So I straightway began the chapter with the London Hospital, and then looked for others to accompany it, nor was there any difficulty in finding them.

The first modest traces of Pears' Soap and Bryant & May have been mentioned elsewhere. Another old friend, whom I was always expecting to find

and never did find for a long time, was Mr. Colman
with his mustard. At last I found him, but not
till 1864 in *Our Mutual Friend*, and then he was
not very picturesque. Still, there he was instead
of a certain Mr. Nunn, who had hitherto apparently been the only mustard maker. And by an
odd chance on the very next page Mr. Keen was
proclaiming his mustard. I suppose one has to
be reasonably old to remember Mr. Keen with his
yellow letters on a black ground as opposed to
Mr. Colman with black letters on a yellow ground.
They seemed romantic once, especially as they
reminded me of the Clare colours at Cambridge,
which I thought very beautiful. There is another
friend of those black and golden days, in which
Mr. Waukenphast, in a tall hat, seemed to cover
the whole side of Cannon Street Station in his
stride. There was "Ozokerit", a name I had not
thought of for ages till I came across it suddenly
in *Edwin Drood*. It seems to have been a fore-
runner of those advertisements of to-day which
keep you on tenterhooks for some days or even
weeks, merely shouting something cryptic at you
and keeping the explanation for another time.
Thus in the sixth number of *Edwin Drood* we find
nothing but "Ozokerit (Patented)" repeated three
times in different kinds of print. There is no clue
as to what "Ozokerit" was. Presumably the clue
was to come later, but this sixth number of *Edwin
Drood* turned out to be the last, and the secret
of Ozokerit was buried with that of John Jasper
and the Princess Puffer and the mysterious Mr.
Datchery who was always patting his hair. Somewhat on the same lines is the cryptic announcement
reproduced here which I take to mean "Titan
Tread."

There are other friends of our youth in the Drood
Advertiser. In the second number there are
Parkins and Gotto, who have set up as rivals to

" There must be something wrong about these Mineral Superphosphates and Oil Cakes. I will try ' THORLEY.' "

" She is quite dry, and not above a Gallon ! "

" Seeing is believing ! I 'll never be led astray any more by reading them high-priced old Agricultural Newspapers."

' Three times the quantity of milk, and much richer in quality, since we tried ' THORLEY.' It proves that a grain of practice is worth a cart-load of Chemistry."

Jaques as makers of croquet sets and will provide the very best box wood set for £3. The mallets had, as I imagine them, tiny little heads, and round the neck of each mallet were stripes of different colours—red and white, blue and white and, most exciting of all, chocolate and white. It was with just such a chocolate and white mallet that I once pursued a young companion all round the lawn with intent to murder. I failed to catch him, but all my teams of imaginary cricketers wore caps of chocolate and white stripes for some time afterwards.

In the same number is to be found "Lamplough's Pyretic Saline." It is sadly dull, however, with one or two mild little testimonials from doctors

TITAN
READ

and not a touch of the flamboyant Enovian genius that was later to put it in the shade.

A far more dashing advertiser is Mr. Thorley of the Cattle Food, who has charming pictures of the farmer, the milkmaid and the cow. I am sure that Dickens himself must have liked those pictures, because they so openly scoffed at science, just as he did himself. His views are, I imagine, accurately reflected in the description of the scientific gentleman in *Pickwick* who wrote a treatise on the lights in his garden, caused by Mr. Pickwick's dark lantern, and told his servant Pruffle he was a fool when he suggested thieves as their origin. I am afraid too that he laughed at dear Mr. Pickwick over the theory of Tittlebats. In the first of the Thorley pictures there is pasted on the cowshed wall a notice that "Professor Bosh prepares reports and analyses to suit the views of the trade." The cow is looking wan and tired, the farmer puzzled, and the milkmaid sad, because the cow "is quite dry and not above a gallon." "There must be something wrong about these mineral superphosphates and Oil Cakes," says the farmer, "I will try 'Thorley'." In the next picture the cow looks a new cow, everyone is radiant and Professor Bosh's placard has been torn down. "Seeing is believing", says the farmer. "I'll never be led astray any more by reading them high-priced old Agricultural newspapers," and the milkmaid rubs it in with, "It proves that a grain of practice is worth a cartload of chemistry."

These views as to the superiority of practice over theory were no doubt shared by the gentleman who wrote to Tidman's Sea Salt about his small daughter. She suffered from a weakness which caused "one of her legs to bow out," but the moment she had a sea-salt bath she could "walk quite strong." So much for doctors!

Apropos of baths, Bath advertises its mineral spa in *Dombey*, despite the fact that Mr. Dombey and Major Bagstock preferred to go to Leamington. There is an imposing picture of the Pump Room, and I think Mr. Angelo Cyrus Bantam himself must have been responsible for the statement that the baths and pump rooms are "the most elegant" in Europe and that the town, "combines all the refined amusements and recreations of the metropolis with the pure and invigorating breezes of the country." The Ilkley Hydropathic advertises in *Little Dorrit*, and so does the Granby Hotel, at Harrogate, "established for almost a century, and well known as a favourite resort of many Families of Distinction." Nowadays these hotels would be eager to point out their facilities for amusements; there would be talk of lawn tennis courts and neighbouring golf courses. The Imperial Hotel, at Exmouth, does hint at archery and croquet, but this is the exception; respectable Podsnappian people who could afford to take themselves and their families to elegant and refined hotels did not play games. Apart from the one or two mentions of croquet I can find nothing in that line except Thurston's billiard tables, which appeared in *Our Mutual Friend*. Whether those respectable people would have played the concertina I am not sure, but at any rate another old friend, Mr. Boosey, thought it worth while to advertise five different brands, the most gorgeous costing twelve guineas made in ebony with plated metal studs. Likewise the "new patent model Cornet-a-Piston introduced by C. Boosé, Bandmaster of the Fusilier Guards," which "produces a beautifully clear and powerful tone and greatly facilitates the execution of the most brilliant music." Mr. Chappell, on the other hand, advertises his twenty guinea pianoforte with check action in *Edwin Drood*, together with every variety of harmonium. A good many of the advertisements in *Edwin Drood* seem, as is only natural, rather modern, for close to Mr. Chappell is Mr. Epps with his cocoa, and Mr. Streeter with his jewellery, and over the page come Mappin & Webb with a charming domestic picture of three ladies drinking electro-plated tea and a parlour maid with cap ribbons bringing in some electro-plated muffins. That is, however, by no means their first appearance; their travelling bags and their epergnes are found in various of the other books.

Beer must certainly be regarded as an old friend, but there is very little about it in any of the Dickens advertisers, although one Felix Summerly made a delightful beer jug from which to drink it, "emblematical of the employment of the hop." He also, by the way, made a mustard pot in porcelain called "The Bitten Tongue" that would have suited Mr. Colman. In one number of *Bleak House* Mr. Allsopp took some eight pages all to himself, but he was far too serious and too indignant to be amusing. It seems that there had been about this time (1852) some reported adulteration of bitter beer; these reports were, according to Mr.

Allsopp, fomented by somebody, "from an unworthy and unneighbourly jealousy" and it was alleged that strychnine was used in the bittering of beer. Mr. Allsopp thought it worth while to attack this report by means of the heaviest artillery he could find and he produced a long letter from Baron Liebig, who said that quarter of a century

DOMBEY & SON ADVERTISER.

FELIX SUMMERLY'S ART MANUFACTURES.

FRANCESCO FRANCIA was a goldsmith as well as a painter. Designs for crockery are attributed to Raffaelle. Leonardo da Vinci invented necklaces. In the gallery of Buckingham Palace is a painting by Teniers to ornament a harpsichord; and in the National Gallery there is one by Niccolo Poussin for a similar purpose. Holbein designed brooches and saltcellars. Albert Durer himself sculptured ornaments of all kinds. At Windsor is ironwork by Quintin Matsys. Beato Angelico, and a host of great artists, decorated books; and, in fact, there was scarcely a great mediæval artist, when art was really catholic, who did not essay to decorate the objects of every-day life. Beauty of form and colour and poetic invention were associated with every thing. So it ought still to be, and we will say, shall be again.

Manufacturing skill is pre-eminent and abounds; but artistic skill has still to be wedded with it. An attempt will now be made to revive the good old practice of connecting the best art with familiar objects in daily use; and this intention will be made manifest by the aid of our best artists, several of whom have already expressed their willingness to assist in this object : among them may be named :—

JOHN BELL, Sculptor.
C. W. COPE, A.R.A.
T. CRESWICK, A.R.A.
J. R. HERBERT, R.A.
J. C. HORSLEY.
S. JOSEPH, Sculptor.
D. MACLISE, R.A.
W. MULREADY, R.A.
R. REDGRAVE, A.R.A.
H. J. TOWNSEND.

The ART MANUFACTURES will be of all kinds, and executed in METALS, WOOD, GLASS, POTTERY, and other materials.

Those now ready are—

A BRIDE'S INKSTAND, price £2 2s., with LETTER-WEIGHT (Kissing Children), 9s., and SEAL-HANDLE, 7s. 6d., to match, designed by John Bell, Sculptor.

A BEER JUG : emblematical of the employment of the hop; designed by H. J. Townsend, price 18s. and 36s. with additional figures.

THE INFANT NEPTUNE, an ornament : modelled by H. J. Townsend, price 27s.

A WATER JUG, in glass, ornamented with enamelled painting; designed by R. Redgrave, A.R.A., price £2 12s. 6d.

A GOBLET, to match, 10s.

THE "BITTEN TONGUE," A MUSTARD POT, in porcelain. Modelled by John Bell, price 9s.

CARVED WOODEN BRACKETS. Designed by S. Delor, in the style of Grinling Gibbons, and executed by Taylor, Williams, and Jordan's machinery, price £5 5s.

DOROTHEA, a Statuette, in Parian. Modelled by John Bell, price £2 2s.

THE MILK JUG which received the Prize awarded by the Society of Arts in 1846. Designed by Felix Summerly; executed in porcelain and glass. Also in silver by Messrs. Hunt and Roskill, 156, New Bond-st.

PURITY, OR UNA AND THE LION, a Statuette. Designed and modelled by John Bell; a companion to Dannecker's Ariadne, or "Voluptuousness," price £3 3s.

"The Lyon would not leave her desolate,
But with her went along, as a strong gard
Of her chaste person."
SPENSER'S FAERIE QUEENE, Booke I., Canto III.

Nearly ready.

A SHAVING MUG, with Brush and Brush-dish, en suite. Designed and ornamented by Richard Redgrave, A.R.A.

A CHAMPAGNE GLASS. Designed and ornamented with gilt enamelling by H. J. Townsend.

A FISH KNIFE AND FORK. Designed by John Bell.

A WINE GLASS AND FINGER GLASS. Designed and ornamented in enamelled colours by R. Redgrave, A.R.A.

A BREAD OR CAKE DISH in glass. Ornamented with gilt enamel by John Absolon.

A NEW SUPPER TRAY in papier mâché, especially for decanters and glasses. Designed and ornamented by R. Redgrave, A.R.A.; with Decanters and Glasses, en suite.

A PAPETIERE. To be executed by Messrs. Jennens and Bettridge.

A BRITANNIA METAL TEA POT. To be executed by Messrs. Dixon, after a design by R. Redgrave, A.R.A.

TWO STATUETTES OF PRAYING CHILDREN, in Parian. Modelled by John Bell; with appropriate Brackets.

A BROWN EARTHENWARE JUG. Ornamented with bas-reliefs emblematical of travelling, by H. J. Townsend.

A SALAD FORK AND SPOON, in wood and ivory, with Bowl, in ruby, glass, &c.

In Preparation.

"THE HAYFIELD," after the Picture by W. Mulready, R.A., exhibited at the Royal Academy in 1847. Painted on a porcelain vase.

A GRATE, with Chimney-piece, Fender, and Fire-irons, en suite—exhibiting a new combination of metal and pottery. The Grate and Fender after the patent of Mr. J. Sylvester.

A Series of DECANTER STOPPERS. Designed by J. C. Horsley.

A DISH FOR THE DRAWING-ROOM, to receive visiting Cards. Designed in colours by D. Maclise, R.A.

AN ARM-CHAIR AND HALL-CHAIR, in wood carving.

The articles are sold by Mr. J. Cundall, 12, Old Bond-street; Messrs. Paul and D. Colnaghi, 13, Pall Mall East; Messrs. Barry and Son, Egyptian Hall, Piccadilly; Mr. G. Bell, 186, Fleet-street; Mr. J. Mortlock, 250, Oxford-street; Mr. J. Phillips, 258 and 259, Oxford-street; Mr. J. Tennant, 149, Strand; Mr. J. Green (late Brumby's), 19, St. James's street; and all respectable dealers.—A Catalogue sent on receipt of a Postage Stamp.

earlier a wicked Westphalian brewer had taken to adulterating his beer with *Nux vomica*. After entirely clearing Mr. Allsopp's character, he gave a handsome testimonial to English brewers in general, and added that to his knowledge the chief brewer of Munich, "who undoubtedly produces the best beer in Germany", had gone through an apprenticeship at Burton. He drank Mr. Allsopp's pale ale himself, and held it to be "a very agreeable and efficient tonic."

One of the numbers of *Little Dorrit* has two whole pages given up to names that are still very familiar. First comes Mudie's Select Library, then Treloar's Cocoanut fibre, with an elegant picture of palm trees, and then Joseph Gillott's Steel pens. Mr. Gillott, who displayed the royal arms as "steel pen maker to the Queen", had a grievance against certain fraudulent persons who had "even copied his name outside their boxes, on which for an obvious purpose is interlined in very small letters the name of a person falsely stated as Late Manager to Joseph Gillott." This wicked person had never done anything to justify this title, and Mr. Gillott accordingly warned his friends against such "equivocal arts." One would imagine that after this everyone must have brought an action against everybody else, but perhaps, as was observed of the mutual threats of Mr. Pickwick and Mr. Magnus, "this sort of ferocity is really the most harmless thing in Nature."

A venerable friend in Mr. Keating, Chemist, has a field day in *Our Mutual Friend*, advertising no less than three remedies. With his "Peruvian Insect Powder" he will destroy the fleas, bugs, flies and beetles that plague us; with his Cough Lozenges he will prevent our having Consumption "of which a cough is the most positive indication" and with his Anthelmintic bonbon or children's worm tablet, he will do what a worm tablet ought to do. The bonbon "dissolves in the mouth like any other sugar plum." I must stop somewhere, and I will stop with Mr. Keating, but Chubb's Safes, Bunter's Nervine, de Jongh's Cod Liver Oil, Kirby's Needles and Pins, triumphant as "the result of litigation," and Letts's Diaries are all there too. So, as far back as *Martin Chuzzlewit*, is "The *Publishers' Circular*, established 1837, new series 1843. Sampson Low." Heal's beds appear regularly, sometimes with a whole back page to themselves, and he also makes the eiderdown quilt which all who have travelled on the Continent know to be "the warmest, lightest and most elegant covering ever introduced." There are many others that must go unsung, and, sometimes in front of them and sometimes behind them, there goes on for ever and ever The Gentleman's Real Head of Hair, or Invisible Peruke.

THE END